KU-270-523

Lee Holmes holds an Advanced Certificate in Food and Nutrition and is a certified holistic health coach (IIN), yoga teacher, wholefoods chef and author of the bestselling titles *Supercharged Food* and *Supercharged Food: Eat Yourself Beautiful*. She is a columnist with *Wellbeing Magazine* and a regular contributor to *Lifestyle Food* (Yahoo), and her articles have appeared in leading Australian newspapers and journals, as well as *The Times* and *The Daily Express* in the UK and *The Huffington Post* in the US. Lee's blog, *superchargedfood.com*, won both the Healthy Eating Category and best blog at the inaugural BUPA Health Influencer Blog Awards in 2013.

*This book is dedicated to all the people
who empower and change the lives of others
through leading by example*

SUPERCHARGED FOOD

EAT CLEAN,
GREEN AND
VEGETARIAN

LEE HOLMES

MURDOCH BOOKS

LONDON BOROUGH OF
WANDSWORTH

9030 00004 1516 2

Askews & Holts	26-Feb-2015
641.5636	£14.99
	WW14005137

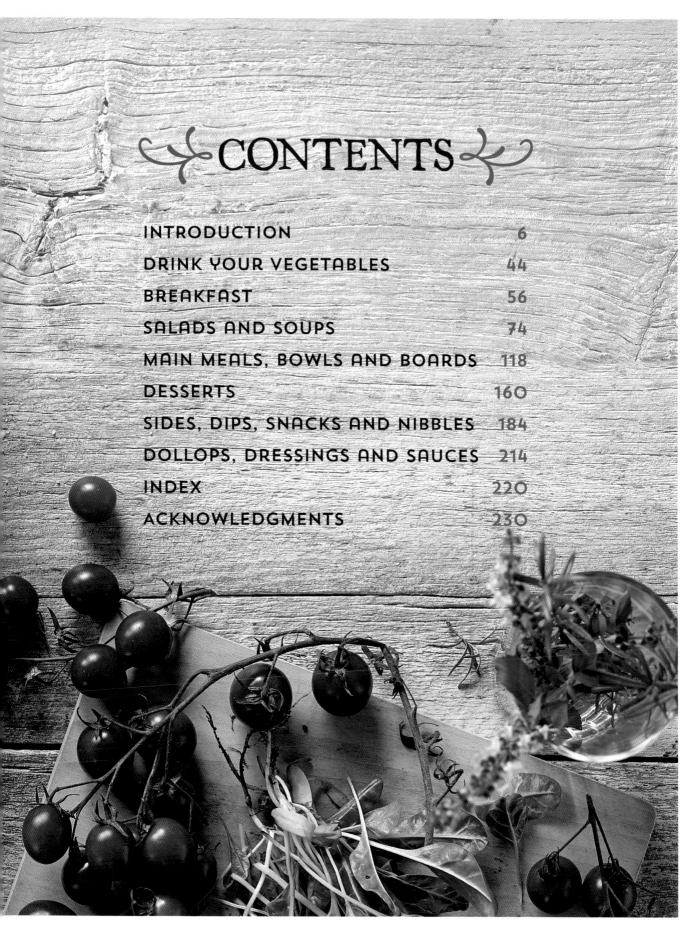

CONTENTS

❧ INTRODUCTION ❧

I grew up in a rickety house on a quarter acre plot in England. Before we had been there a year, my mother had transformed it from an uncultivated, bramble-infested wilderness to a beautiful vegetable garden into which we would disappear, emerging with purple-stained hands triumphantly clutching fistfuls of rhubarb, or carrying makeshift buckets, bursting with juicy seasonal berries.

Growing our own fruit and vegetables and having an edible garden as kids was not only intensely satisfying, it also taught us about nature, the changing seasons and the cycle of life. We watched seedlings poke their first tentative leaves out of the earth, harvested them and enjoyed them for our dinner. It was profoundly nourishing, not only gastronomically but also metaphysically.

Being responsible for creating your own produce means you know exactly what goes into your meals and you can choose the produce that you like to eat, cook and nourish your body with. 'Organic' and 'buying local' have slipped into the current lexicon, and to my mind, there's nowhere more local than our own backyards (or window box or patio or balcony).

I moved to Australia and, after careers in the media and music industries, I went back to my food and nutrition roots to become a wholefoods chef, hatha yoga teacher and certified health coach (Institute Integrative Nutrition).

This is my fifth book, the four earlier books being *Supercharged Food: Eat Your Way to Good Health* and *Supercharged Food: Eat Yourself Beautiful* (Murdoch Books) and *Supercharged Food for Kids* and *Heal Your Gut*, ebooks available on my website, superchargedfood.com. My first book came about after I successfully used nutrient-rich ingredients and wholefoods as medicine to overcome an auto-immune disease and fibromyalgia.

One of my favourite pastimes is creating healthy and delicious recipes. I hope the recipes in this book inspire you to view your ingredients and fresh seasonal produce in a new light and see how the humble vegetable, with a little culinary care, can be the hero of the dinner table.

ABOUT THIS BOOK

Supercharged Food: Eat Clean, Green and Vegetarian features a host of plant-based recipes. Whether you're a vegetarian, vegan or flexitarian, the recipes may be adapted and you can experiment and substitute ingredients depending on your individual preferences and eating guidelines. Eating clean and green will also help you get lean, and that is a bonus. Hello, meat-free everyday!

This is not a vegan cookbook, but all recipes contain vegan options. See page 37, Veganising and Healthy Swaps, for more information.

Much of the hyper-processed food available in our supermarkets has been technically engineered to increase yield (and profits), regardless of the effects this has on our health or the environment. Eating real, whole, unprocessed and nutrient-rich food is the best health insurance policy we have. This book is more than a collection of vegetable recipes – you will find no hockey-puck veggie patties or nut roasts within these pages. It will inspire you to create thoroughly delicious meals loaded with nutrients and health-promoting properties to supercharge your health.

GUIDE TO ICONS

WF DF GF SF VEG VG

The following icons appear with each recipe. Here's a breakdown of what each signifies.

WF: WHEAT-FREE. For some people, wheat is hard for their sensitive guts to digest and can cause allergic reactions. Common symptoms of a wheat allergy can include eczema, hives, asthma, hay fever, Irritable Bowel Syndrome (IBS), tummy aches, bloating, nausea, headaches, joint pain, depression, mood swings and tiredness. Wheat products can be replaced with buckwheat, rice, quinoa, tapioca and wheat-free flours.

DF: DAIRY-FREE. To avoid dairy, look on labels for any food that contains cow's or goat's milk, cheese, butter, ghee, buttermilk, cream, crème fraîche, milk powder, whey, casein, caseinate and margarines which contain milk products. Substitutes for dairy milk include rice milk, nut and seed milks, oat milk and coconut milk.

GF: GLUTEN-FREE. Gluten is a mixture of proteins found in grains such as wheat, rye, barley and oats. Some people can tolerate oats but the tricky bit is finding oats that are uncontaminated by wheat or other grains during processing. Symptoms of gluten sensitivity can include gastrointestinal issues, skin problems, changes in weight, headaches and depression. Gluten sensitivity can make you feel ill or uncomfortable and can adversely affect your mood and quality of life.

SF: SUGAR-FREE. Sugar provides energy without nutrients. Researchers have reported that a person with vitamin and mineral deficiencies, such as magnesium, zinc, fatty acids and B-group vitamins, is more likely to show symptoms of anxiety and depression. In this book, if a recipe contains fruit, coconut sugar or rice malt syrup I have indicated that it contains sugar, and therefore it doesn't appear with the sugar-free icon.

VEG: SUITABLE FOR VEGETARIANS. If you're vegetarian, it's a good idea to include forms of protein, iron, vitamins B12 and D and calcium in your diet to ensure you're eating enough essential nutrients. Good fats from non-meat sources are also very important. Eating a wide variety of real foods and avoiding cutting out wholefood groups unless absolutely necessary is a philosophy which works well for many people long-term.

VG: SUITABLE FOR VEGANS. These meals contain no meat, fish, shellfish or any product made using any part of any animal, including sea-creatures, milk, cream, yoghurt, butter, cheese, eggs and honey. If the recipe is not marked as vegan, there will be an option for you to veganise it.

ALL ABOUT VEGETABLES

Vegetables are the edible parts of plants, including the leaves, roots, tubers, flowers, stems, seeds and shoots. Legumes are the pods, fruit or seeds of the plant and may be eaten in their immature form, as green peas and beans; and also in mature form, as dried peas, beans, lentils and chickpeas.

Generally vegetables are low in fat, high in fibre and contain essential vitamins, minerals and antioxidants. If you were to sum up a group of vegetables by nutritional profile, you would commonly find that green leafy vegetables are great sources of vitamin C. For vitamin A, munch on the dark green leaves from leafy vegetables such as spinach and broccoli (and I promise you that the recipes within won't taste like lawn clippings!) Add orange vegetables such as carrots and pumpkin (winter squash) to your dishes, too. Pregnant women who need a lot of folate in their diet will find it in abundance in green vegetables, dried peas and beans. You'll also find small but significant quantities of iron, calcium and phosphorus in your favourite vegetables, too.

One way to classify vegetables is by their plant origin, such as roots, stems or leaves and flowers,

fruits or seeds. The following is a list of popular vegetables, broken up into groups. I have placed each vegetable into their primary category, but they may fall into more than one. (For example, onions are listed as a root vegetable but they could also be classified as a stem vegetable.)

ROOT

bamboo shoot	parsnip
beetroot (beet)	potato
carrot	radish
cassava	salsify
celeriac	shallot
daikon	swede (rutabaga)
garlic (bulb)	sweet potato
ginger	taro
horseradish	turmeric
Jerusalem artichoke	turnip
jicama	yacon
onion (bulb)	yam

STEM / LEAF

asparagus	leek
broccoli	lettuce
Brussels sprouts	pak choi
cabbage	parsley
cauliflower	radicchio
celery	rhubarb
chard	rocket
chicory	Savoy cabbage
Chinese cabbage	silverbeet (Swiss chard)
endive	snow peas
fennel	spinach
kale	watercress
kohlrabi	

FLOWER / FRUIT / SEED

artichoke	pepper
beans	pumpkin (winter squash)
broad (fava) beans	runner beans
cucumber	soy beans
eggplant (aubergine)	squash
French beans	sweet chestnut
lentils	tomato
marrow	zucchini (courgette)
peas	

THE HEALING PROPERTIES OF VEGETABLES

It's time to embrace life-changing luscious vegetables as a healing instrument in your life. By now, we all know that the key to good health is a balanced diet, minimising stress levels, looking after your emotional wellbeing and regular stretching and exercise. But sometimes it's hard to figure out what exactly constitutes a balanced diet. There's so much conflicting advice from experts and dieticians, and even recommended daily allowance amounts that were previously based on averages are falling short of our body's actual nutritional needs. It's easy to make the leap once you know how.

To achieve a balanced diet, you should be consuming a variety of whole, unprocessed foods that provide an adequate proportion of protein, carbohydrates, fibre, fat, vitamins, minerals and water. Focusing on the nutrients that you need in optimal amounts and eating in moderation will enable your body to function at its best without any futzing around.

Over the past year I've been fasting two days per week and have found it enormously helpful for my health and energy levels. 'Fasting' doesn't entail cutting out food altogether (collective sigh of relief), but rather limiting kilojoule (calorie) intake to 2500 kilojoules (600 calories) for men and 2100 (500) for women. The great thing about fasting days is that you can consume a delicious array of vegetables in good quantities and they not only fill you up, but provide you with many necessary vitamins and minerals to make you feel fantastic.

You don't need to love yoga, kale and horsetail braids to enjoy a vegetarian diet. Let's get ourselves acquainted with the curative values of delicious vegetables and enjoy the essential nutrients that they provide. It's difficult to argue with the amazing benefits of dark green, red, yellow and orange vegetables. These vegetables are rich sources of calcium, magnesium, potassium, iron, beta-carotene, vitamins B-complex, C, A and K, and will have your body jumping for joy.

Consuming just four cups of veg a day will provide you with plenty of soluble and insoluble fibre and a boost of plant sterols, which are an effective way to lower low-density lipoprotein (LDL) (bad) cholesterol in the bloodstream by interfering with cholesterol absorption in the small intestine. LDL cholesterol can lead to the build-up of plaque in arteries (atherosclerosis), a contributing factor in heart disease and strokes.

Vegetables are rich in antioxidants, which protect the human body from oxidant stress by boosting immunity and fighting disease. They also have a mellowing effect on blood sugar levels, which can in turn help keep your appetite in check.

There are *so* many reasons to increase our vegetable intake. Here are five simple reasons to include vegetables in your daily diet.

VEGETABLES MAKE YOU BEAUTIFUL FROM THE INSIDE OUT

We live in a world obsessed with beauty, and we're bombarded by advertisements for products that claim to hold the key to youth and gorgeousness. But beauty doesn't have to cost you the world – it can be found by simply adding the right foods to your grocery list. After all, beauty is an outward expression of what is going on inside. You can cake your face with lotions, potions, concealers and foundations, or you can experience the natural glow that comes from eating a diet rich in vegetables in a rainbow of colours.

Research published in *The Journal of Public Health* concludes that carotenoids, a phytonutrient found in red, yellow and orange vegetables, creates a 'glow' in the skin that is perceived as more attractive than a tan. Carotenoids are found in carrots, red capsicum (pepper) and pumpkins (winter squash).

Eating a wide variety of coloured vegetables is the key to keeping yourself looking good and feeling great. An abundance of phytonutrients will act as powerful antioxidants that will protect your skin cells from premature aging and damage from UV rays, as well as providing anti-inflammatory benefits.

⁓ Supercharged Tip ⁓

Did you know that red capsicums (peppers) protect the skin's DNA and collagen, and are also highly detoxifying?

VEGETABLES ARE OBESITY'S ARCH ENEMY

I'm sure you're all aware that the West is in the middle of an obesity epidemic. We have a diet that favours processed foods, animal products and sugar. An increased vegetable intake is proven to correlate with lower rates of obesity and related chronic diseases.

Vegetables are so low in kilojoules, it's difficult to gain weight even if you eat mountains of them. Nuts have an array of amazing health benefits, although it's important to remember that they are energy-rich, typically containing 15 times the amount of kilojoules of their veggie friends. This is not a reason to boycott nuts – as with so many things in life, balance is the key. But in the modern age, this 'balance' has been warped. Our diets are heavily weighted with kilojoule-rich foods, when the majority should be made up of vegetables.

Just to be crystal clear, I'm not talking about the canola oil-slathered, cooked-to-near-death and smothered-in-cheese kind of vegetable. Nor am I talking about the cup-a-soup, boxed or tinned varieties that claim to have 'five veg in one serve'. These are lifeless, rubbish-filled mimics of the real deal. What you need is an abundance of fresh vegetables, preferably seasonal and organic, to ensure you're getting maximum nutrition, minus any nasty chemicals – and the taste will really knock your socks off.

VEGETABLES ARE HIGH IN FIBRE, WHICH IS ESSENTIAL FOR DETOXIFICATION

Fibre is something that we all need more of and veggies have a whopping amount. If your toilet trips are floundering, you may just need to up your veggie intake. While it may not be a table topic you care to ponder, it really is important to be aware of how many trips you make to the bathroom each day. Eliminating the bowel is our body's most obvious way of removing waste and toxins, so if it isn't happening very often, it means that you are holding on to bacteria in the walls of your intestinal tract. Experts say that once a day is the minimum requirement for your toilet trips, and the evacuation should be brief and effortless.

When our digestive system slows down, our body's response is to protect itself from the accumulated toxins in our tissues by surrounding them with a layer of fat and mucus. It's said that an accumulation of 2–9 kilograms (5–20 pounds) of encrusted, putrefying faeces is not uncommon in the Western population. Over time, these deposits increase and are leached into the bloodstream. This is where symptoms of illness arise.

Indigenous cultures that traditionally have a high intake of vegetables, and therefore dietary fibre, enjoy superior intestinal health and are virtually free of the intestinal diseases of many modern civilisations. Eating a diet high in vegetables gets this elimination pathway working optimally; speeding up the passage of food residue through the digestive tract. This will also lower your risk of colon cancer, and decrease the absorption of toxins from stools.

VEGETABLES ARE MUCH LOWER IN FRUCTOSE THAN THEIR FRUITY FRIENDS

While fruit is glorious in taste and high in nutrients, most fruits are also high in fructose. Unfortunately, the argument that eating an abundance of fruit will provide you with all your nutritional needs is a bit of hogwash. In fact, you're probably doing your body more harm than good if you are eating too much fruit.

Did you know that table sugar contains 50% fructose, and a banana contains 55% fructose? Fructose is a type of sugar that is converted directly to fat, and that is not recognised by our system, meaning that we need to eat a lot of fruit to feel full. This is bad news for your weight.

The human body has only been designed to tolerate one to two small pieces of fruit a day, maximum, and just one glass of apple juice, fresh or otherwise, contains the equivalent of 10–12 teaspoons of sugar. If you're going with fruit, get sugar-savvy and indulge in all types of berries, lemons, limes, nectarines, grapefruit, guava and avocado. It only takes a few small dietary tweaks to get the best out of the foods you are eating.

Astonishingly, most packaged foods, breads and just about everything in the modern diet contains added sugar in the form of fructose. So, thinking fruit can substitute vegetables is not going to benefit your health. The high fructose content causes an acidic digestive tract where illness can thrive, increases inflammation, suppresses the immune system and destabilises the body's homeostasis.

Vegetables, on the other hand, are bursting with just as many nutrients as fruit, but are significantly lower in fructose. Hello new bathing suit!

❧ Supercharged Tip ❧

Get your digestive system moving by munching on more vegetables. High-fibre veggies include peas, artichokes, parsnips, green leafies, Brussels sprouts, fennel and turnips. You're going to fall in love with the fragrant Curried Parsnip Soup recipe on page 112.

VEGETABLES ARE NINJAS AGAINST DISEASE

Want to turn your body into an environment where chronic disease wouldn't dare set foot? Eating oodles of veggies is the first step. For example, cruciferous vegetables like kale, collard greens and broccoli are known to be serious cancer fighters. They're super-high in antioxidants, making them wonderful for preventing inflammation, and they scavenge on the free radicals which lead to the growth of cancerous

cells. A wonderful anti-inflammatory dish is the Indian Whole Roasted Cauliflower on page 208. I eat this dish on a weekly basis.

Green vegetables are also bursting with chlorophyll. Chlorophyll is the molecule that absorbs sunlight and uses its energy to synthesise carbohydrates from carbon dioxide and water; a process also known as photosynthesis. This fascinating property is also wonderful when consumed through your veggies, as it oxygenates the blood, improves circulation, reduces DNA damage, fights infection, is anti-carcinogenic, and detoxifies the body of heavy metals.

Vegetables are also highly alkalising. A highly acidic environment is where illness will be having a field day, and eating a diet loaded with raw veg, especially green vegetables, is a surefire way to keep your acid/alkaline balance just right.

Juicing is one of the best ways that you can increase your veggie intake and experience their alkalising benefits. Fresh vegetable juices are full of living enzymes, vitamins, minerals and antioxidants that will give your body the best support to keep its healing systems working optimally, ward off chronic disease and provide you with loads of energy. If you're wondering where to start, then why not begin by incorporating a Raw Superfood Greenie Smoothie from page 48 into your weekly routine. You'll start to feel wonderful almost instantly.

NUTRIENTS NEEDED FOR OPTIMAL HEALTH

The levels of vital nutrients needed vary depending on our state of health, lifestyle and age, and so standard recommended daily allowances (RDAs) shouldn't be taken as gospel. Vegetables assist in a release of energy provided by the carbohydrates, fat and protein we consume. Vitamins come in two types: water- or fat-soluble. Fat-soluble vitamins are stored in the liver and include vitamins A, D, E and K. Water-soluble vitamins, which our bodies are not able to store, include B-complex and C.

If you're a vegetarian, it's vital to consume enough vitamin B12, which is responsible for red blood cell growth and nervous system maintenance, but is only required by the body in small amounts. The RDA for healthy adult males and females is 2.4 micrograms (mcg) of vitamin B12, but remember that RDAs can vary from person to person. You can find B12 in foods such as nutritional yeast flakes, eggs, milk and cheese.

❧ Supercharged Tip ❧

How to drink your minerals: Caffeine reduces your body's ability to absorb calcium, as well as stimulating the release of stress hormones and aggravating anxiety. If you're looking to replace coffee, I've concocted a beautiful Vegan Chai Dandy recipe (see page 49). It contains cardamom, a spice from the evergreen rainforests of Southern India, and a great source of minerals like iron, manganese, potassium, calcium and magnesium. It's the perfect drink to have as a warmer through the winter months.

Your body needs 16 essential minerals. Some, such as calcium, are needed in large amounts and others, like selenium, are needed in smaller quantities. Different minerals perform different functions, but most importantly they regulate the body and maintain a healthy immune system.

Calcium is important for bone and overall health, and RDAs for adults 18 to 50 years old are 1000 milligrams (mg) per day, while those 51 and older should consume 1200 mg daily. If you don't consume milk or dairy products, you can increase your calcium intake by eating more chickpeas, broccoli, dried figs, wholemeal bread, orange juice or cereal. Vitamin D, found in eggs, cereals and butter, as well as sunlight, assists with calcium absorption.

ESSENTIAL VITAMINS AND MINERALS

VITAMIN	BEST VEGETARIAN SOURCES	ROLE IN HEALTH	DEFICIENCY
Vitamin A (Retinol in animal foods, beta-carotene in plant foods)	Milk, butter, cheese, egg yolks, fatty fish, seaweed, yellow–orange vegetables and fruits such as carrots, pumpkin (winter squash), mango, sweet potatoes, apricots and other vegetables such as red capsicum (pepper), green leafy veg, spinach and broccoli	• maintains normal reproduction • maintains healthy vision • formation and maintenance of healthy skin, teeth and soft tissues of the body • beta-carotene acts as an antioxidant and protects the immune system	Poor night vision, dry skin and lower resistance to infection, especially in the respiratory tract
Vitamin B1 (Thiamine)	Wholegrain breakfast cereals, baking flour, whole grains, wheat germ, brewer's yeast, legumes, nuts, potatoes, pulses, nutritional yeast flakes, quinoa, seaweed and peas	• essential for energy production to tissues • good for the nervous system and nerve function, the muscles and heart • helps break down and use the energy and nutrients in carbohydrates, proteins and fats • promotes growth and boosts mental ability	Depression, irritability, nervous disorder and loss of memory
Vitamin B2 (Riboflavin)	Milk, eggs, cheese, yoghurt, almonds, pepitas (pumpkin seeds), fortified breads, breakfast cereals, nutritional yeast flakes, almond milk and seaweed	• obtains energy from food • makes vitamin B6 active in the body • reduces a key cardiovascular risk factor • produces red blood cells and body growth	Lack of energy, dry cracked lips, numbness and itchy eyes
Vitamin B3 (Niacin)	Pulses, potatoes, beans, wholegrain cereals, eggs, cheese, milk, peanuts, wheat germ, mushrooms, nutritional yeast flakes, green leafy veg, figs, prunes, tamari and quinoa	• obtains energy from food • breaks down and uses carbohydrates, proteins and fats and their building blocks • maintains healthy skin and nerves • releases calcium from cellular stores	Lack of energy, depression and scaly skin
Vitamin B5 (Pantothenic acid)	Potatoes, oat-based cereals, tomatoes, egg yolks, whole grains and seaweed	• hormones, vitamins A and D and substances that help make nerves work • helps make new fats and proteins in the body	Fatigue, apathy, numbness, cramps, insomnia and rheumatoid arthritis
Vitamin B6 (Pyridoxine)	Eggs, wholemeal (whole-wheat) bread, fortified breakfast cereals, nuts, bananas, broccoli, cabbage, cauliflower, Brussels sprouts, green peas, beans, split peas, fruit and quinoa	• breaks down, uses and re-forms the building blocks of proteins	Anaemia, dermatitis and depression

VITAMIN	BEST VEGETARIAN SOURCES	ROLE IN HEALTH	DEFICIENCY
Vitamin B12 (Cyano-cobalamin)	Nutritional yeast flakes, eggs, milk and cheese	• normal nerve function • normal blood function	Fatigue, increased risk of infection and anaemia
Folate (Folic acid)	Green leafy vegetables, bread, nuts, pulses, bananas, cereals, broccoli, legumes, eggplant (aubergines) and oranges	• breaks down and uses the building blocks of proteins • the processes of tissue growth and cell function • maintains good heart health • prevents neural tube defects in newborns	Appetite loss and anaemia
Biotin	Breakfast cereals **Note:** eating raw egg whites prevents absorption of biotin	• breaks down and uses the building blocks of fats and proteins	Dermatitis, pins and needles, anaemia, depression and conjunctivitis
Choline	Milk, eggs, peanuts, wheat germ and dried soy beans	• makes nerve cell transmitters and cell membranes • inflammatory and allergic response • healthy kidneys and liver • reduces the risk of heart disease • fat and cholesterol transport and breakdown in the body	Fatigue, insomnia and memory problems
Vitamin C (Ascorbic acid)	Citrus fruits, blackcurrants, guava, kiwi fruit, melons, raspberries, tomatoes, capsicum (pepper), broccoli and sprouts	• protects against oxidative damage • aids absorption of iron and copper • formation of collagen • healthy bones • helps fight infection • helps regenerate and stabilise other vitamins such as vitamin E or folate	Increased susceptibility to infection, fatigue, poor sleep and depression
Vitamin D	Sunlight on skin allows the body to produce vitamin D; eggs, cereals and butter	• absorbs calcium and phosphorus • maintains calcium levels in blood • healthy immune function • healthy skin • promotes muscle strength	Softening of the bones, muscle weakness and anaemia
Vitamin E (Tocopherol)	Seeds, nuts, wheat germ, oats, spinach, cashews, peanuts, almonds and sunflower seeds	• acts as antioxidant particularly for fats • keeps heart, circulation, skin and nervous system in good condition	Increased risk of heart attack, strokes and certain cancers

Continued overleaf

VITAMIN	BEST VEGETARIAN SOURCES	ROLE IN HEALTH	DEFICIENCY
Vitamin K (Phyllo-quinone)	Spinach, salad greens, cabbage, broccoli and Brussels sprouts	• normal blood clotting	Uncontrollable bleeding and bruising
Calcium	Milk, cheese, yoghurt, bony fish, legumes, fortified soy beverages and fortified breakfast cereals. **Note:** The body excretes calcium with salt in urine, so eat less salt to retain your calcium	• develops and maintains bones and teeth • good functioning muscles and nerves • heart function	Soft and brittle bones, osteoporosis, fractures and muscle weakness
Chromium	Widely found in foods such as eggs, whole grains and cheese	• enhances the action of insulin to regulate blood sugar	Impaired glucose tolerance, weight loss, nerve damage and confusion
Copper	Nuts, seeds, wheat bran cereals, buckwheat and whole grains	• the functioning of several enzymes • forms connective tissue • iron metabolism and blood cell formation • nervous system, immune system and cardiovascular system function	Anaemia and muscle weakness
Iodine	Saltwater fish, shellfish, seaweed, iodised salt and vegetables (if there is iodine in the soil where they are grown) **Note:** Severe deficiencies can cause miscarriage, stillbirth, infant mortality and congenital abnormalities	• normal thyroid function (important in the growth and development of the central nervous system) • energy production • oxygen consumption in cells	Sluggish metabolism, dry skin and hair, and formation of goitres
Iron	Wholegrain cereals, buckwheat, coconut flakes and almond milk **Note:** Iron absorption from plant sources e.g. cereals or green leafy vegetables is much lower than from animal sources, so 80% more is required in the food to get the same amount absorbed. Vitamin C helps with iron absorption	• haemoglobin in red blood cells (important for transport of oxygen to tissues) • component of myoglobin (muscle protein)	Anaemia, fatigue and low resistance to infection
Magnesium	Green vegetables, legumes, peas, beans, lentils, nuts, whole grains, buckwheat and cereals	• aids the function of more than 300 enzyme systems • energy production • regulates potassium levels • the use of calcium • healthy bones	Lethargy, weak muscles and bones, depression and irritability

VITAMIN	BEST VEGETARIAN SOURCES	ROLE IN HEALTH	DEFICIENCY
Manganese	Cereal products, tea, tamari, buckwheat and vegetables	• healthy bones • carbohydrate, cholesterol and protein metabolism	Poor glucose tolerance, nausea, vomiting, hearing loss, bone loss, loss of hair colour, fainting, irritability and skin rashes
Molybdenum	Legumes, wholegrain products and nuts	• breakdown of proteins	Malfunction of the liver, jaundice, nausea and fatigue
Phosphorus	Widely distributed in natural foods e.g. dairy, meat, dried fruit, eggs and cereals	• forms part of DNA and RNA • buffers the acidity of urine • protects the acid/base balance of blood • storage and transport of energy • helps activate some proteins	Muscle weakness, confusion, seizures and coma
Potassium	Leafy green vegetables, tomatoes, cucumbers, zucchini (courgette), eggplant (aubergine), pumpkin (winter squash) and root vegetables. Also present in beans, peas, bananas, avocados, buckwheat, milk and yoghurt **Note:** Potassium has a beneficial effect in offsetting the effects of sodium (salt) on blood pressure	• nerve impulses • muscle contraction • regulates blood pressure	Weakness, thirst, fatigue, mental confusion and raised blood pressure
Selenium	Seafood, poultry, eggs and, to a lesser extent, other muscle meats and cereal foods (content varies widely with soil condition)	• antioxidant • thyroid metabolism • part of several functional proteins in body	Reduced antioxidant protection
Sodium	Found in most takeaway and processed foods e.g. bread, butter, cheese and cereals. It is also a major component of table salt and baking soda **Note:** It is important to use only moderate amounts of salt as recommended in the dietary guidelines	• maintains water balance throughout the body • nerve impulses • transports molecules across cell walls	Dehydration, cramps and muscle weakness
Zinc	Cereals, coconut flakes, buckwheat, pepitas (pumpkin seeds) and dairy foods **Note:** Availability from animal sources is greater than that from plant sources, so vegetarians need 50% higher intakes	• component of enzymes that help maintain structure of proteins and regulate gene expression • needed for growth, immunity, appetite and skin integrity	Impaired growth and development, slow wound healing and loss of taste and smell

Iron is required for red blood cell formation and cellular metabolism. Drinking coffee and tea, particularly with meals, can limit your iron absorption so the best time to drink them is at least three hours before a meal. If you're looking for an injection of iron, try fresh tofu, lentils, green leafy vegetables, chickpeas and hummus. Vitamin C increases the absorption of iron, so if you take an iron supplement, it's a good idea to eat berries or vitamin C–rich foods at the same time. Copper helps the body absorb iron – foods containing high levels of copper include oysters, shellfish, dark green leafy vegetables, dried legumes, nuts and chocolate. Yes, I said chocolate!

ORGANIC VERSUS CONVENTIONAL

If you chat with anyone who works in the organic farming industry, they'll tell you that their produce is much better for you nutritionally than conventionally grown fruit and vegetables. Organic produce is fruit and vegetables that are free from artificial fertilisers, herbicides and pesticides. Rather than relying on chemicals, organic produce is grown in harmony with nature, using natural methods of pest and disease control to harness and maintain soil fertility. The number one reason people have turned to organic food is for health reasons, and their concern about the use of chemicals in its production. The Organic Federation of Australia has a number of studies and reports on the higher nutritional content of organic foods and also non-organic produce and the effect that eating it has on your health.

A certified organic product is far more than just chemical-free. It's also a demonstration of how the farmer has grown and handled the produce from paddock to plate, from soil to plantation and its environment. The standards for organic certification are internationally recognised, and all certified farms and organic products are subject to annual audits by independent third parties.

If you aren't in a position to grow your own, then eating more locally grown fruits and vegetables will support your local economy and farmers. It makes sense to try and source your produce close to home, as less energy is used to get these products to the local market than those grown elsewhere, making it better for the world, as well as your health.

> The greatest delight the fields and woods minister is the suggestion of an occult relation between man and the vegetable. 'I am not alone and unacknowledged.' They nod to me and I to them.
>
> RALPH WALDO EMERSON

SO WHY BUY ORGANIC?

One compelling reason to buy organic wherever possible is to limit your own chemical exposure. Several commercial pesticides and herbicides have been linked to cancer, birth defects, nerve damage and genetic mutations. When you really think about it, it makes sense that a poison designed to kill a living organism would also affect a human detrimentally.

If you enjoy the taste of fresh produce, then you'll notice a difference in the taste of organically grown fruit and vegetables. That's because organic farming begins its journey in well-nourished soil. This in turn increases the nutrient content of the plant, and eventually changes our palate.

Let us all encourage biodiversity. Conventional farming methods often rely on monoculture, the planting of the same crops year after year. This method of farming reduces the quality of the soil as the same crop extracts and uses the same minerals every day, resulting in farming practices that rely on a host of chemicals in order to artificially nourish and support the development of a crop. Accordingly, the conventional produce we buy lacks vital nutrients and contains residual chemical

fertilisers with minimal living nutrients. Why support agribusiness and factory-produced food when we can support our own organic farmers who practise crop rotation, allowing the soil to naturally replenish and restore itself?

If you're finding it difficult to locate a local source, the big supermarkets now have large organic lines at very affordable prices so you don't need to spend a week's wages on organic food. There are also hundreds of online organic delivery businesses that will deliver fresh, local, organic vegetables straight to your door. The local farmers' market is another good way to get the highest-quality veg, and most sellers are at least chemical-free. By getting to know your grower, you can discover the process that your food has gone through. Purchasing this way will also mean that the produce hasn't travelled over continents to get to your shopping trolley. For more information on sourcing vegetables, see page 29.

With the average child being exposed to more cancer-causing pesticides in their food (here's the research: nrdc.org/health/kids/ocar/chap5.asp), your smart food choices today can help determine the future health of generations to come.

CLASSIFYING VEGETARIANS

You obviously don't have to be a vegetarian to enjoy vegetarian food. Not a vegetarian myself, I classify myself a flexitarian, meaning that while I eat a lot of vegetables and enjoy a plant-based diet, I also eat small quantities of sustainably produced meat, as I find it lessens the symptoms of my auto-immune disease. With this book, I hope to encourage people to eat more vegetables and be inspired to blaze their own healthy trail, whatever that may be.

There are many different kinds of vegetarians, and most vegetarians and mainstream vegetarian diets can be divided into the following categories:

- **Ovo lacto vegetarian** is perhaps the most common form of vegetarianism. This involves eating no meat, fish or any product made using any part of any animal, including fish and other sea creatures. However, ovo lacto vegetarians do eat products derived from live animals, for example dairy products (such as milk, cream and cheese) and eggs.

- **Veganism** is where no meat, fish or any product made using any part of any animal, including fish and sea creatures, or products derived from animals, is eaten.

- **Lacto vegetarians** avoid meat or fish products and eggs, but dairy products such as milk, cream, cheese, ice cream and yoghurt are eaten.

- **Ovo vegetarians** stay away from meat, fish and dairy products such as milk, cream and cheese. Ovo vegetarians do eat eggs though.

- **Pesco vegetarian** (also called pescatarian) is an eating philosophy where meat or any product made using any part of any land-animal, including poultry and other birds, is avoided, but dairy products such as milk, cream, cheese and eggs, and fish and sea creatures such as shellfish and crustaceans, are consumed.

- There are also people who partake in a vegan **raw food diet** which consists of unprocessed vegan foods that have not been heated above 46°C (115°F). Raw foodists believe that foods cooked above this temperature have lost a significant amount of their nutritional value.

- The **macrobiotic diet**, revered by some for its healthy and healing qualities, includes unprocessed vegan foods, such as whole grains, fruits and vegetables, and allows the occasional consumption of fish. Sugar and refined oils are avoided. Perhaps the most unique qualifier of the macrobiotic diet is its emphasis on the consumption of Asian vegetables, such as daikon, and sea vegetables, such as seaweed.

No matter what your eating principles, the recipes in this book can be adapted to your own tastes and philosophies. I hope that they will become your heirloom recipes, ones that you can repeat again and again and pass down through the family.

LETTING MORE VEGGIES INTO YOUR LIFE

Get ready to leap into the green zone. Here are eight quick tips to packing more bright, crisp vegetables into your life.

1   Pre-prepare and trim, roast and chop them up into bite-sized pieces ready for eating. That way you'll be more likely to grab lunch on the go or snack on a celery stalk or kale chip. Yes please!

2   Keep them out on the counter or top and centre in the fridge. Crisper draws are always well hidden – make your veggies the first thing you see when you open the fridge door.

3   Make your veggies a meal and have them take centre stage. Choose vegetables you're unable to resist. That way you'll want to indulge often. Even serve them with a crunchy salad.

4   Drink your vegetables – juice them up or make them into a green smoothie with the addition of avocado. You won't be disappointed. If you want to add sweetness, use coconut water as your mixer.

5   Swap out wraps, breads and crackers for vegetables instead. Use lettuce leaves when making san choy bow and tacos, wrap sandwich and Mexican fillings in kale and leafy greens.

6   Explore your local market, green grocer or produce aisle and choose something new. Bring some variety into your life and try a new veggie like daikon or kale.

7   Have your own box of mixed vegetables delivered each week. It forces you to get more creative and let nothing go to waste.

8   Find innovative ways to add more vegetables to your meals. You could top your gluten-free pizza with kale, or throw spinach into a green pasta sauce and serve with zoodles (see the recipe on page 111). Add one more vegetable to your meal at breakfast, something that is not traditionally a breakfast food. For example, you might like to try the Green Breakfast Bowl on page 66 – it's a perfect starter for the day ahead.

MY TOP TEN SUPERCHARGED VEGETABLES

Rustling up a sumptuous vegetarian meal with amazing vegetables from your garden or fridge will provide you with good nutrition, stable blood sugar levels and long-term health benefits. It's a good idea to go for a variety of produce, colours, shapes and sizes to give your body the mix of nutrients it needs. I like to go for dark leafy greens, and rich tones of yellow, orange, red and purple.

KALE is the queen of greens, containing more calcium than milk and more iron than beef per kilojoule. A great detoxifier, kale is filled with fibre and sulphur – vital for a healthy liver and digestive system. Add to that a healthy dose of omega-3s and kale becomes the ultimate anti-inflammatory supercharged ingredient. Try it sautéed in a stir-fry, raw in a salad or sprinkled with olive oil and baked in a hot oven for a crispy chip treat!

SPINACH One cup of spinach contains almost 20% of your daily recommended intake of dietary fibre, aiding digestion, maintaining low blood sugar and keeping you feeling fuller for longer. Spinach is high in flavonoids, a phytonutrient that has been shown to slow down cell division of cancer cells in the body. Spinach can be eaten raw in salads, or stirred through a curry at the last minute for an extra nutrient kick. And if you have a fussy eater, blending spinach into a yummy breakfast smoothie can be a great way to sneak veggies into their diet.

ZUCCHINI (COURGETTE) is filled with amazing nutrients including vitamins C and A, potassium, folate and fibre – all of which contribute to a healthy heart by reducing the risk of stroke, preventing high blood pressure and lowering cholesterol. Get the most from your zucchini by slicing it into fine noodles and enjoying in a raw salad, baking coin-shaped discs with olive oil into crunchy perfection, or try grated zucchini in cookies and breads for added moisture. There is a fantastic Baked Zucchini Fries recipe on page 186, and it's one that you can make your own by varying the spices used.

CAULIFLOWER Humble it may be, but it is full of vitamin C, a vital antioxidant for boosting immunity and protecting against cancer. It is also a wonderful source of potassium and rich in the mineral boron, which assists in the development of lean muscle. Cauliflower is truly versatile: it can be used as an alternative to mashed potato, a dairy-free option to add richness to soups instead of cream, or as the ultimate low-starch side when chopped into florets and sautéed to resemble fried rice. I like to make 'popcorn' by chopping florets into small pieces and baking them with olive oil, turmeric, lemon and garlic.

GREEN BEANS contain an array of nutrients including protein, fibre, calcium and iron. One cup of raw green beans has more than 200 milligrams of potassium as well as beta-carotene and vitamin A. Beta-carotene may reduce some forms of cancer and vitamin A assists your body to maintain healthy eye and bone status. Enjoy green beans raw or blanched in salads, grilled with olive oil or as a perfect crudités vessel for homemade guacamole. Slow-cooked green beans are delicious and you'll find a Slow-Cooked Green Beans recipe on page 205.

AVOCADO Beautiful, rich, creamy and filled with vital monounsaturated fat, avocado slows digestion and helps stabilise blood sugar. As well as increasing feelings of fullness, the oleic acid in avocados may assist in lowering cholesterol levels. Half an avocado also contains over 3 grams of both soluble and insoluble fibre, which your body needs to keep the digestive system running smoothly. Try mashing it into a chunky guacamole with tomatoes, coriander and spices. Alternatively, avocado can be blended with raw cacao and stevia for a sugar-free, nutrient-intense chocolate mousse. I always use a dollop of creamy avocado dressing with my Muchos Nachos on page 125.

TURNIP This oft forgotten nipper is an exquisite alternative to starchy potatoes. One cup of mashed turnips contains about 27 mg of vitamin C, which helps to support tissue repair and immunity. Turnips also provide several B vitamins, including riboflavin, thiamine, niacin, folate and pantothenic acid. All these B vitamins help with fat, carbohydrate and protein metabolism; nervous system function; and maintaining healthy skin, hair, eyes and liver, and are often missing in the vegetarian diet. Consider slicing turnips into batons and frying like chips, or cubing and adding to your favourite slow-cooked casserole or curry.

BROCCOLI has a truly remarkable nutritional profile. It contains high levels of both soluble and insoluble fibre and is a rich source of immune-boosting vitamin C. In fact, 100 grams of broccoli will provide you with 150% of your recommended daily intake. Broccoli is a delicious and nutritious side to any family meal. Blanch a few heads at the beginning of the week and add to your salads or serve as a side with a lashing of lemon juice and cracked Celtic sea salt. Don't forget the stalk either. Purée steamed broccoli stalks with tahini, garlic and olive oil for a different take on hummus or add to stir-fries for bulk and crunch.

DAIKON A longstanding member of the radish family, daikon is an excellent source of fibre, vitamin C, phosphorus and potassium. When cut into wafer-thin slices, daikon is a delicious raw accompaniment to a heavy meal, with natural enzymes that aid the digestion of fat and carbohydrates. Daikon Ravioli? Turn to page 156 to see how this is possible.

FENNEL Touted for its benefits to the digestive system, its medicinal properties have been well documented. Iron and histidine are two interesting amino acids found in fennel, both of which stimulate the production of haemoglobin, a useful treatment for anaemia and an often-lacking nutrient in many vegetarian diets. I love fennel sliced thinly into salads or braised in olive oil and lemon juice and added to a hearty seafood soup. Remember not to waste the green tip fronds; it is a great fresh aniseed-like herb that looks resplendent as a garnish on any dish. Fennel also tastes delectable baked as Sea-Salted Fennel Chips (see page 190).

SEASONAL GUIDES

AUSTRALIA

SPRING artichoke, asparagus, avocado, beans, broad (fava) beans, broccoli, cabbage, carrot, cauliflower, cucumber, leek, lettuce, peas, potato, radish, rhubarb, rocket (arugula), silverbeet (Swiss chard), snow peas (mangetout), spinach, sugar snap peas, sweet corn, tomato, zucchini (courgette)

SUMMER asparagus, avocado, borlotti beans, capsicum (peppers), celery, chillies, cucumber, eggplant (aubergine), fennel, globe artichokes, green beans, leek, lettuce, okra, peas, potato, radish, snow peas, squash, sugar snap peas, sweet corn, tomato, zucchini

AUTUMN Asian greens, avocado, beans, beetroot (beets), borlotti beans, broccoli, Brussels sprouts, cabbage, capsicum, carrot, cauliflower, celery, cucumber, eggplant, fennel, garlic, kohlrabi, leek, lettuce, mushrooms, onion, parsnip, peas, potato, pumpkin (winter squash), shallot, silverbeet, spinach, squash, swede (rutabaga), sweet corn, sweet potato, tomato, turnip

WINTER Asian greens, avocado, beetroot, broccoli, Brussels sprouts, cabbage, carrot, cauliflower, celeriac, celery, fennel, horseradish, Jerusalem artichoke, kale, leek, okra, olives, onion, parsnip, peas, potato, pumpkin, silverbeet, spinach, swede, sweet potato, turnip, witlof (chicory/Belgian endive)

UNITED KINGDOM

SPRING asparagus, beetroot, broad beans, broccoli, Brussels sprouts, cabbage, cauliflower, celeriac, garlic, kale, leek, lettuce, morel mushrooms, onions, peas, radish, rhubarb, rocket, spinach, spring greens, swede, watercress

SUMMER artichoke, asparagus, aubergines, beetroot, broad beans, broccoli, cabbage, carrot, cauliflower, celery, courgettes, cucumber, fennel, french beans, leek, lettuce, new potatoes, onion, peas, peppers, radish, rhubarb, shallots, spinach, tomato, turnip

AUTUMN artichoke, aubergine, beetroot, Brussels sprouts, cabbage, carrot, cauliflower, celeriac, celery, courgettes, cucumbers, florence fennel, french beans, kale, lettuce, mushrooms, parsnip, peas, peppers, potato, pumpkin and squash, radish, shallots, spinach, swede, sweet corn, tomato, turnip

WINTER broccoli, Brussels sprouts, cabbage, carrot, celeriac, celery, kale, leek, lettuce, parsnip, pumpkin, spinach, swede, turnip

UNITED STATES

SPRING artichoke, arugula, asparagus, beets, broccoli, butter lettuce, celery, collard greens, kale, lettuce, peas, peppers, rhubarb, snow peas, spring onions, spinach, Swiss chard, turnip, watercress

SUMMER arugula (limited availability), beets, bell peppers, cabbage, carrot, cauliflower, celery, chayote squash, cucumber, eggplant, endive, french beans, garlic, green beans, jalapeño peppers, lima beans, manoa lettuce, okra, onion, peas, peppers, potato, radish, shallots, spinach, summer squash, sweet corn, Swiss chard, tomatillo, tomato, turnip, winged beans, zucchini

FALL acorn squash, arugula, beets, broccoli, Brussels sprouts, butter lettuce, buttercup squash, butternut squash, celeriac, celery, endive, fennel, garlic, ginger, green beans, kale, kohlrabi, leek, lettuce, mushroom, onion, peas, peppers, potato, radicchio, squash, sweet potato, Swiss chard, turnip

WINTER beets, Belgian endive, broccoli, Brussels sprouts, butternut squash, cabbage, carrot, cauliflower, celeriac, celery, collards, curly endive, fennel, kale, leek, lettuce, onion, parsnip, potato, radish, rutabaga, shallots, spinach, squash, sweet potato, Swiss chard, turnip, winter squash

SOURCING VEGETABLES AND PRODUCE

If you're not growing your own, shopping for your cornucopia of fresh vegetables has never been easier, and you don't need to spend a lot of money to get the cream of the crop. From farmers' markets to supermarkets, vegetables are making their way from the paddocks and fields onto stalls and shelves across the country. Over the last couple of years we've seen a dramatic increase in the availability of a wide variety of vegetables in more mainstream areas, and nutritious glowing and organic produce is far more accessible for the everyday consumer.

If you're on a budget, buy in bulk and in season when produce is abundant. Many farmers' markets, greengrocers and health food stores have an area where you can buy in bulk and they frequently offer large discounts on seasonal or locally grown produce. Check supermarket flyers for vegetables and produce that may be on special from week to week.

Here are my top five ways to find the best quality healthy produce.

VISIT A PRODUCE STAND OR FARMERS' MARKET

Depending on where you live, you should be able to find a seasonal or weekly farmers' market near you (see page 30 for more details). Farmers' markets are a great way to meet the growers and sellers of organic fruits, vegetables, free-range eggs, spices, herbs and other produce such as dressings and condiments. As produce comes directly from the source, prices are generally more affordable. It's a good idea to allow yourself a little bit of extra time when you go to a produce market to browse and chat with farmers about their products, so you can understand the journey of the food you are eating and how it was produced.

> *A man taking basil from a woman will love her always.*
>
> SIR THOMAS MOORE

(see page 30 for more details)

Supercharged Tip

If you're not on a budget but you're time-poor, invest in fresh vegetables that are pre-washed and sliced. They can be added directly to any recipe or eaten as a quick snack, and having them on hand encourages you to eat well.

GET IN TOUCH WITH YOUR LOCAL HEALTH FOOD STORE OR CO-OPERATIVE

Health food stores and co-ops are great places to discover healthy items that can't be found in your local supermarket. To find your nearest store, try the Australian Organic Food Directory (organicfooddirectory.com.au), which provides listings of organic retailers, community food systems and farmers' markets. If you're in the UK, visit nahs.co.uk, and if you live in the USA, visit the Eat Well Guide at eatwellguide.org. If you're having trouble finding a particular item, most health food stores and co-ops are happy to fill special orders.

DISCOVER YOUR NEAREST COMMUNITY FOOD SYSTEM

Community food systems include community-supported agriculture, box schemes where you can order a box of fresh produce weekly, co-operatives, farmers' markets and community gardens. Get in touch with your nearest community food system and support the change to more sustainable food and ways of living.

VISIT AN ETHNIC GROCER

Ethnic grocers are a wonderful way to discover new flavours and tastes to enhance your meals. There are many Asian grocers selling exotic fruits and vegetables, seaweeds, stocks, sauces and medicinal teas at lower prices than some health food stores. Middle Eastern and Greek grocers are a fantastic source of new flavours, such as hummus, tahini, baba ghanoush, falafel, grape leaves, olives and condiments. Jewish or kosher stores also carry a variety of dairy-free items.

GO CYBER, BUY ONLINE

If you're having trouble sourcing a health food store in your area, there are a number of online stores where you can buy a range of produce and ingredients which are delivered straight to your doorstep. Look for an online store in your state so you are cutting out air miles, and get involved in their holistic food system and rewards programs.

ꞏ Supercharged Tip ꞏ

If you have children, take them with you to do the vegetable shopping. Letting them pick their own vegetables makes the shopping trip fun, and they'll be more likely to eat the produce if they've had a hand in picking it themselves.

THE DIRTY DOZEN

Every year, the Environmental Working Group (EWG) ranks supermarket produce by its pesticide level. The highest offenders become the 'Dirty Dozen', and are the fruits and vegetables you should consider buying organic. If you cannot afford to buy organic for all the foods you consume, consider at least buying organic versions from the following list. It's good to bear in mind that the information provided by the EWG's Shopper's Guide to Pesticides in Produce is based on produce bought at supermarkets. Choosing to shop at your local farmers' market gives you the opportunity to ask the farmers about their growing practices. While they may not be certified organic, they may still farm in a sustainable manner, using few to no pesticides. The choice is yours, but the relationship between farmer and buyer is paramount to fresh, seasonal and local produce.

THE DIRTY DOZEN

apples	hot peppers
capsicum (peppers)	nectarines
celery	peaches
cherry tomatoes	potatoes
cucumbers	spinach
grapes	strawberries

The Environmental Working Group has also created a clean fifteen list to help you shop smarter, which includes the following produce:

CLEAN FIFTEEN

asparagus	mushroom
avocado	onion
cabbage	papaya
canteloupe (rockmelon)	pineapple
eggplant (aubergine)	sweet corn
grapefruit	sweet peas
kiwi fruit	sweet potato
mango	

ꞏ Supercharged Tip ꞏ

If you're not technically challenged, go online to find guides to your local farmers' markets.
farmersmarkets.org.au (AUS)
localharvest.org (USA)
localfoods.org.uk (UK)

STORING YOUR VEGETABLES

No-one likes to open the fridge to find limp and sad-faced vegetables (#saynotolimpgreens!) Different vegetables need different storage conditions to slow down their deterioration. The main factors to consider are temperature and humidity. Because the water content of fruits and vegetables is high, even small percentages of moisture loss can result in limp and unappealing produce. Look on pages 33–4 for a handy guide to storing your veg. Pop this on your fridge to help save you time and money.

REFRIGERATOR TIPS

Before storing your vegetables, wash and dry all leafy matter so it is ready to be cut, steamed, sautéed or eaten straight from the fridge. This is a lifesaver during busy working weeks. Once you have washed and dried them, store them in the fridge wrapped in paper towels to preserve their shelf-life. Avoid washing mushrooms and delicate herbs as it will only make them spoil quicker and turn into sludge.

When storing vegetables, ensure that you remove ties and elastic bands and trim off any leafy ends. If you're storing them in plastic bags, make sure that there is good circulation of air by piercing holes in the bag, and pack the vegetables loosely. The more crowded your produce is, the shorter its shelf-life.

Do not store fruits and vegetables together. The majority of fruits emit high levels of ethylene, which prematurely ripen surrounding vegetables.

METHODS OF COOKING FOR OPTIMUM NUTRITION

Vegetables contain enzymes that both make and destroy vitamins. After your produce has been harvested, the production of vitamins stops, but the degradation continues. Apart from buying fresh, local and in-season produce, there are some wonderful methods to use to cook your vegetables to ensure optimum nutrition.

BLANCHING is a method of pre-cooking vegetables so that they only need reheating later. Blanching vegetables prior to freezing is vital, as this destroys certain enzymes and bacteria and helps preserve the colour and texture of your vegetables. To blanch your vegetables, bring a pot of water to a rolling boil, add the vegetables, and bring back to the boil for a few minutes only. Drain, and then immerse the vegetables in ice-cold water immediately. When the vegetables are cold, thoroughly dry, then freeze. Simply reheat in boiling water when ready to serve.

STEAMING maintains the flavour, nutrition and minerals in your veggies. To enhance the flavour of steamed vegetables, add slivered garlic to your steamer or slices of fresh ginger to the boiling water to infuse the vegetables with their aroma.

SAUTÉING is quick and easy. Stir-frying vegetables means cooking them over high heat, stirring frequently. The intense heat means your vegetables are not cooked for long, reducing mineral loss.

PICKLING is an age-old method of preserving foods for a long period without refrigeration. It is usually done using a combination of salt, acid and/or fermentation. The process of fermentation is not only a great way of preserving food, but also boosts the vitamin content of the vegetables. Eating fermented vegetables ensures you get your daily dose of dairy-free gut-healthy probiotics.

DEHYDRATING is the act of removing water from foods at a slow, controlled rate in order to preserve the maximum amount of enzymes and nutrients. Modern methods use an electronic dehydrator or a conventional oven set at the lowest temperature to ensure that precious vitamins and minerals are not lost in the 'cooking' process. This both increases the food's longevity and ensures it has a similar nutritional profile to its fresh counterpart.

ROASTING involves very little preparation. Just toss your chosen vegetables in a good quality olive oil, add some dried herbs or spices for flavour, place them in a baking dish and roast. This gives you more time to invest in your main meal and is a great way of using up older vegetables in the fridge.

A HEALTHY PANTRY

Creating a healthier lifestyle is a gradual process and one of the best places to start is in the pantry. But don't worry, you don't need to do it all at once! Making small and consistent changes every day will lead to big changes in your life. As your items run out each week, replace them with healthier options. If an item is not past its use-by date, but you know that you won't eat it, donate it to your local charity. Imagine opening the doors to a fully stocked kitchen cupboard, and revealing an array of wonderful food choices to make you feel energetic and superhuman. Stocking your pantry with these staples will ensure that you're always prepared for every eventuality.

When you're in need of some inspiration, have these key go-to ingredients stocked in your pantry. They partner well with vegetables and can be used to add nutrition, flavour and bulk to your veggie dishes. Ingredients so good, they deserve a cape!

QUINOA is derived from the seed of a plant that is related to spinach; it's highly nutritious, gluten-free, a good source of iron and protein and provides a dose of healthy fats. It is a pure protein, which means it contains all of the essential amino acids your body needs to build muscle. Quinoa contains an amino acid called lysine, as well as vitamin B6, thiamine, niacin, potassium and riboflavin. It also provides your body with copper, zinc, magnesium and folate. Add it to breakfast porridge, salads and soups, or serve as a side with savoury main meals.

COCONUT FLAKES are a metabolism booster and a great source of fibre and healthy fats. They're a fantastic hormone balancer, too, and contribute to a happy and healthy thyroid. Coconut is a good source of iron and zinc, a mineral crucial to the strength and health of your immune system. Sprinkle coconut flakes on desserts to enhance the flavour, or add to breakfast cereals.

NUTRITIONAL YEAST is a deactivated yeast, often a strain of *Saccharomyces cerevisiae*. It's a great source of B-complex vitamins and is a complete protein. Add a tablespoon to stir-fried vegetables, use in baking or sprinkle on top of soups. This may sound a bit off-the-wall, but I like to make 'Vegemite' from yeast flakes; I blend them with butter and then slather it on spinach toast.

BUCKWHEAT boasts myriad health benefits. It contains the eight essential amino acids, several minerals including zinc, iron, manganese, potassium, phosphorus, copper and magnesium, and is high in B vitamins that are essential to energy production and the optimal functioning of your digestive system. Add it to salads and breakfast bowls, or serve as a side to main dishes.

FLAXSEEDS are a natural source of alpha-linolenic acid, one of the primary omega-3 fatty acids, a powerful anti-inflammatory. Flaxseeds contain insoluble dietary fibre, help in the promotion of more regular bowel movements and remove toxins from the body, promoting digestive health. Add a tablespoon of seeds to smoothies, or sprinkle ground flaxseeds into cereals, soups, homemade baked goods or scatter on top of vegetables. Flaxseed oil also tastes delicious on salads.

SUNFLOWER SEEDS contain bone-healthy minerals such as calcium, magnesium and copper. They are also a good source of vitamin E, which eases arthritic pain. Use them in baking, eat them as a snack or lightly toast and sprinkle onto a salad.

GINGER contains potent anti-inflammatory compounds called gingerols. These substances, when taken regularly, help people who suffer from inflammatory conditions such as osteoarthritis or rheumatoid arthritis. Use in stir-fries to pump up the flavour, or add to breakfast, drinks or baking.

SEAWEED helps alkalise the body, and wakame seaweed is an excellent source of vitamins A, B1, B2, B3, B5, C, E, K, folate and soluble/insoluble fibre. Seaweed has a high amount of anti-inflammatory omega-3 EPA essential fatty acid. Roll up your vegetables in seaweed and get a powerful dose of essential nutrients.

PEPITAS (PUMPKIN SEEDS) are rich in zinc, vital for the immune system and wound healing. Use them in granola, cereals and baking, add them to a trail mix or toss them into a salad.

VEGETABLE	BEST STORAGE METHOD	FRIDGE	SHELF LIFE
alfalfa	Store in a paper bag or a container	Yes	3–4 days
artichoke	Store in the fridge	Yes	1–2 weeks
asparagus	Wrap the ends in damp paper towel or stand in 1 cm (½ inch) of water and cover with a paper bag	Yes	2–3 days
beans	Store in the fridge, can also be frozen	Yes	7 days
bean sprouts	Store in a paper bag or a container	Yes	3 days
beetroot (beets)	Cut the leaves 5 cm (2 in) above the root for longer shelf life	Yes	2–4 weeks
bok choy	Store unwashed in an airtight container	Yes	5 days
broccoli	Mist heads and store wrapped in paper towel	Yes	5–7 days
Brussels sprouts	Take sprouts off the stalk, leaving outer leaves intact. Store in the fridge in a bowl or an unlidded storage container	Yes	7 days
cabbage (cut)	Trim outer leaves and store in a bag in the fridge	Yes	7 days
capsicum (pepper)	Store wrapped in paper towel or in airtight bag in the crisper	Yes	5–7 days
carrot	Remove the leaves and tips and store in a covered container filled with water	Yes	1–2 weeks
cauliflower	Remove the leaves, turn head downwards and store in an airtight paper bag	Yes	5–7 days
celery	Store wrapped in foil or paper towel	Yes	1–2 weeks
Chinese broccoli	Store wrapped in a paper bag in the crisper	Yes	3 days
choko	Store in a cool, dry, well-ventilated space for longer shelf life	Yes	10 days
choy sum	Store in a paper bag in the crisper	Yes	5 days
corn	Leave husks on, store wrapped in damp paper towel in the coolest part of the fridge. Loses sweetness over time	Yes	7 days
cucumber	Store on top shelf in fridge: if too cold, chilling injuries result, including water-soaked areas, pitting and accelerated decay. Also accelerates fruit decay and dehydrates easily	Yes	7 days
eggplant (aubergine)	Bruises easily, dehydrates easily. Store at room temperature in a vented bowl. It can be kept in the refrigerator for 1–3 days if used soon after removal	Yes	3 days
endive	Remove damaged leaves before storing	Yes	1–2 weeks
fennel	Store in an airtight container in the fridge	Yes	7 days
garlic	Store bulbs whole in a cool, dry, dark place	No	2 months
ginger	Freeze for up to 3 months or store in ziplock bags in the fridge	Yes	1–2 weeks
herbs	Use quickly, trim stems and stand in 2 cm (¾ inch) of water	Yes	5 days

Continued overleaf

VEGETABLE	BEST STORAGE METHOD	FRIDGE	SHELF LIFE
kale	Store in paper towels in the fridge	Yes	3–5 days
kohlrabi	Remove leaves and stems before storing	Yes	1–2 weeks
leek	Trim and store in a sealed container or bag	Yes	2–3 weeks
lettuce	Store rolled up in paper towel. Use as soon as possible	Yes	5–7 days
mushroom	Store in a paper bag or wrapped in a dry, clean cloth in the crisper to prevent sweating and drying out	Yes	2–3 days
okra	Store in a paper bag or dry, clean cloth in the crisper	Yes	2 weeks
onion	Store in a cool, dry, dark place, away from root vegetables	No	2 months
parsnip	Remove leaves and store in a cool, dark place, or in the crisper wrapped in paper towel. Can be frozen	Yes	3–4 weeks
peas	Leave in pods	Yes	3–5 days
potato	Store in a cool, dry, dark place, without plastic	No	3–4 weeks
pumpkin (winter squash) (cut)	Remove seeds and store in the crisper	Yes	5 days
pumpkin (winter squash) (whole)	Store in a cool, dry, dark place	No	2 months
radish	Remove leaves, store in a paper bag in the fridge	Yes	1–2 weeks
shallots	Store with ends wrapped in damp paper towel	Yes	3–5 days
silverbeet (Swiss chard)	Store in a sealed container in the crisper	Yes	3–5 days
snow peas (mangetout)	Store in a zip-lock bag or sealed container in the crisper	Yes	2–3 days
spinach	Store wrapped in paper towel in the fridge	Yes	3 days
squash	Store in a cool, dark, dry place	No	3 weeks
swede (leaves) (rutabaga)	Trim leaves off root before storing	Yes	3 days
swede (root) (rutabaga)	Trim leaves before storing	Yes	2–3 weeks
sweet potato	Store in a cool, dry, dark place. Sensitive to chilling	No	3–4 weeks
turnip (leaves)	Trim leaves off root	Yes	3 days
turnip (root)	Trim leaves before storing	Yes	2 weeks
watercress	Store in a bowl with 1 cm (½ inch) of water and cover in plastic	Yes	3–4 days
zucchini (courgette)	Store in a paper bag in a dry place	Yes	1–2 weeks

TAMARI is a healthy gluten-free alternative to soy sauce. Tamari has several unexpected health benefits, providing niacin, vitamin B3, manganese and protein, as well as the essential amino acid tryptophan, which contributes to the production of serotonin, known to stabilise mood and promote healthy sleep. Use tamari to add a salty flavour to dishes, add to dressings and dips, shake it onto steamed vegetables or use it as a cooking 'oil' for vegetables such as mushrooms and kale.

EXTRA VIRGIN OLIVE OIL is richly endowed with a unique combination of monounsaturated fats, polyphenols and phytosterols. It's a good choice for bolstering the immune system and helping to protect against viruses. Look for cold-pressed extra virgin olive oil, which is healthier and has a fuller flavour. Heat, light and air can affect the taste of olive oil and its health-promoting nutrients. It's a good idea to store olive oil in a cool, dark place and use it within two months of opening. Use as a dressing or in dips, and remember not to heat it too high as it has a low burning point.

COCONUT OIL is a healthy saturated fat that supports immune system function. It contains lauric acid, which is a proven antiviral, antibacterial and antifungal agent that is easily digested. It helps the body eliminate toxins as well as improving digestion and the absorption of beneficial nutrients. The best coconut oil is one that is cold- or expeller-pressed and unrefined. It's a safe oil to use for cooking as it has a high burning point. Virgin coconut oil becomes cloudy below 24°C (75°F) and solid below 18°C (64°F). To melt it, place the container in warm water. Enhancing the natural flavour of foods, its consistency and great taste make it ideal to use when sautéing or frying or with curries and Thai-style dishes. You can also use it in desserts and baking.

TAHINI is made from sesame seeds that have been soaked and crushed. It has a high healthy oil content, filled with omega-3s and omega-6s. Spread on gluten-free crackers or combine with olive oil and lemon juice to create a creamy salad dressing. You can also add it to desserts and puddings.

APPLE CIDER VINEGAR is made from apple juice that's been fermented twice, once to hard apple cider and then a second time to become apple cider vinegar. It can be used as a health tonic, a cure for hiccups and to promote digestion, as well as a beauty aid and a household cleaner. Look for it raw, organic, unfiltered and unpasteurised to use in your recipes. Add zing to your vegetables, use it as a marinade, pickle with it, add it to salad dressings or substitute it when a recipe calls for vinegar.

ALMOND MILK is good to have on hand if you need a dairy-free milk alternative. And it's nourishing too, containing 50% of the recommended daily requirement of vitamin E and potent antioxidant properties essential for skin health. It's also full of B vitamins and minerals such as iron and riboflavin, both important for muscle growth and healing. Make your own, or you can find almond milk in most supermarkets. Ensure that you check for additives, sugar and unhealthy oils. Use on cereals, in baking and as an alternative to milk.

COCONUT WATER is the liquid found inside young, green coconuts. I use coconut water to sweeten up vegetables when stir-frying. Add it to green vegetable smoothies or enjoy as a drink on its own. Use it to sweeten your dishes and beverages.

CHIA SEEDS are a great source of essential fats and high in dietary fibre, making them great for digestion. Chia is a complete protein containing eight essential amino acids. Sprinkle them onto breakfast dishes, soups and salads. Add them to bread and muffin recipes. You can also use chia as an egg replacer by mixing the seeds with water or coconut water to form a thick gel.

RICE MALT SYRUP can be used in the same ratio as sugar and has the sweetness of caramelised honey. Rice malt syrup is made by culturing rice with enzymes to break down the starches. The mixture is then cooked until it becomes a syrup. Unlike fructose, it provides a steady supply of energy into the body due to the mixture of complex carbohydrates, maltose and a small amount of glucose.

VEGANISING AND HEALTHY SWAPS

Just because you're eating a plant-based diet doesn't necessarily mean that the processed soy, meat and dairy alternatives you find in your local supermarket are healthy. Your diet should focus on wholefoods that are as close to their natural state as possible. The recipes in this book are all able to be veganised, and the alternative ingredients are nutritious as well as convenient.

If you're craving a snack, keep healthy bites on hand so you're not tempted by processed food. Start reading food labels, and if they look like they're written by a mathematician or scribed in a foreign language, then give them a wide berth. Cleaning out your pantry is a good place to start, and investing in kitchen gadgets, such as a vegetable spiraliser, mandolin or food processor, make it easy to rustle up delicious vegan meals.

Some of the best ways to veganise a meal are to use the swap-out system.

DAIRY ALTERNATIVES

Swap cow's milk for seed or nut milks such as almond, cashew, Brazil nut or hazelnut. Nut milks are a healthy option as they are high in calcium and good fats, and are easy on the digestive system. There are a variety of non-dairy milks springing up on supermarket shelves, such as ancient grain milk and rice milk, among many others. You can also use full-fat and additive-free coconut milk or cream as a dairy replacement in your cooking.

A good supplement to use instead of butter is coconut oil, a heart-healthy oil bursting with good fats to regulate your cholesterol levels. You can also use light olive oil or grapeseed oil in baking instead of butter at the same ratios, but keep in mind that grapeseed oil can cause inflammation so is best avoided if you can find an alternative. For slathering on toast, coconut butter, tahini and avocado are great alternatives to butter.

Use nutritional yeast flakes instead of cheese. Nutritional yeast is a deactivated yeast made from a single-celled organism, *Saccharomyces cerevisiae*, which is grown on molasses and then harvested, washed and dried with heat, making it non-active. It's left with no leavening ability, but the good news is that no animals were harmed in its making. You can find it in your health food store and it comes in flakes and powder form. If you're intending to use the powder, you'll need to halve your quantities as it is more concentrated. Nutritional yeast, as its name implies, is packed with nutrition, loaded with B vitamins, folic acid, selenium, zinc and protein. It's a great addition to a vegan diet as it contains vitamin B12, which is absent from plant foods unless it has been added as a supplement.

There are certain inhibitors present in soy that block protein and nutrient absorption and which can cause abdominal distress in some people, so it is best to stay away from cheese alternatives such as GM soy and GM soy–based products. Be on the lookout for soy protein, soy bean oil or soy lecithin, an emulsifier that's added to many processed foods. Soy bean oil is another additive which is generally derived from genetically modified soy beans. It's common in foods like mayonnaise and salad dressings, and supplemented in baked goods such as breads and cakes. Textured vegetable protein (TVP) contains the flavour enhancer MSG, which can bring on unpleasant reactions in some people, especially those allergic to soy.

If you do like soy, proceed with caution, and ensure that you eat it in its whole, organic and fermented state, by eating products such as miso, tempeh and tamari in moderation.

If you're looking for a cheese substitute, you can go right ahead and make your own cashew nut cheese, which is a healthy and delicious alternative and works well on pizzas.

Hummus made from chickpeas, tahini, olive oil, garlic and lemon can be used as a cheese-like condiment to go with falafels, or thinned out to be used to replace cheese sauces or mayonnaise. Or flick over to the Cashew Dressing recipe on page 219.

EGG ALTERNATIVES

Eggs have a couple of functions when it comes to baking. They can act as a binder to hold the recipe together, or as a leavening agent to help it rise (and sometimes they take on both roles at once). Determining their role in a recipe will help you to ascertain which replacement options are the best for the recipe.

There are a number of egg replacers you can buy in supermarkets made up of ingredients like potato starch, tapioca flour, calcium carbonate, and additives such as citric acid, vegetable gum (stabiliser) and methylcellulose or cellulose gum. This is a polymer that comes from the cell walls of woody plants, which works as a thickening agent, stabiliser and emulsifier. It can be found in a multitude of products, from shampoos to ceramics to ice cream. Your body isn't able to properly break down cellulose gum, so it passes through your digestive tract and isn't absorbed into your bloodstream.

SIX EASY WAYS TO ADD THE BENEFITS OF COCONUT OIL TO YOUR DAILY DIET

1 Add a tablespoon of coconut oil to your favourite breakfast smoothie or hot drink.

2 Add a tablespoon to amaranth porridge with a drop of stevia or a drizzle of rice malt syrup.

3 Spread on crackers or gluten-free bread instead of butter.

4 Use coconut oil for your stir-fries and curries — it works wonderfully with Asian and Indian flavours.

5 Roast vegetables with coconut oil and Celtic sea salt — simple yet delicious.

6 Mix coconut oil with raw cacao powder and rice malt syrup for a delicious, healthy chocolate topping or dipping sauce.

If you have time, I suggest you use real food as a natural egg replacer and make your own. Here are some swap-outs you can make.

If you're cooking or baking, then the following substitutes can be used, for one egg:

- 1 tablespoon ground or whole chia or flaxseeds soaked in 60 ml (2 fl oz/1/4 cup) of water for 15 minutes. Allow it to rest until it becomes gelatinous
- 1/4 cup mashed ripe banana, mashed avocado, cooked pumpkin (winter squash), apple sauce or puréed fruit
- 2 tablespoons arrowroot powder
- 1 cup nut milk plus 1 tablespoon apple cider vinegar
- 2 tablespoons water mixed with 1 tablespoon light olive oil and 2 teaspoons additive-free baking powder

To help recipes rise, substitute one egg with the following:

- 1 teaspoon additive-free baking powder mixed with 1 tablespoon water and 1 tablespoon apple cider vinegar
- 1 1/2 tablespoons oil mixed with 1 1/2 tablespoons water and 1 teaspoon baking powder. Mix until it fizzes and then add it to the recipe

Gelatine replacers:

- 1 tablespoon of agar agar powder plus 1 tablespoon of water. Mix, place in fridge and then mix again

NUT ALTERNATIVES

If you can't handle nuts, then use seeds instead. Packed with vitamins, minerals and essential fatty acids, these plant-based pocket rockets help boost immunity and energy. Try pepitas (pumpkin seeds), sesame, sunflower, chia and flaxseeds in and on your dishes. Seeds are rich in magnesium, manganese and omega-3 fatty acids that aid in maintaining a healthy digestive system.

If you're investigating crunchy toppings, you can use toasted coconut flakes, dulse flakes or kale chips, or scatter over some nutritional yeast to give foods a cheesy nutty flavour. I can't think of a reason not to get involved with these bonus superfoods.

When baking, try a gluten-free flour such as buckwheat flour, which is rich in magnesium, manganese and tryptophan. Coconut flour is a good alternative, but ensure you add extra liquid as it does absorb more liquid than traditional flours. Brown rice flour, quinoa, tapioca and arrowroot are all good nut-free and gluten-free flour substitutes and can add a textural component to a dish.

SHOPPING LIST

If you arrive at the store without a plan, then fear not — head straight to the produce section and start building your weekly menu according to what is in season, what looks ravishing and flourishing and what works within your own budget. If the mushrooms look appealing and you buy them in bulk, plan to stuff them and bake them on Monday night, cook them up with other veg in a stir-fry on Tuesday night, and add them to a casserole on Wednesday night. Here's a comprehensive list to get you started.

VEGETABLES

Asian greens	chillies	pumpkin (winter squash)
asparagus	cress	rocket (arugula)
avocado	cucumber	shallots
beetroot (beets)	daikon	silverbeet (Swiss chard)
bok choy	eggplant (aubergine)	snow peas (mangetout)
broccoli	fennel	spinach leaves
Brussels sprouts	garlic	spring onion
butternut pumpkin (squash)	green beans	sprouts (all)
cabbage	kale	swede (rutabaga)
capsicum (pepper)	lettuce greens	sweet potatoes
carrots	mushrooms	tomatoes
cauliflower	olives	turnip
celeriac	onions	watercress
celery	parsnips	zucchini (courgette)
cherry tomatoes	peas	

EGGS (ORGANIC)

eggs

DAIRY (FULL FAT)

organic butter	sheep's cheese	full-fat plain yoghurt, no additives
organic cream	full-fat cheese	
goat's cheese	parmesan cheese	

FATS AND OILS

coconut oil (extra virgin)	seed and nut oils	butter
extra virgin olive oil (cold-pressed)	sesame oil	

SEEDS, NUTS AND NUT BUTTERS

almond
Brazil
hazelnut
macadamia
pecan

walnut
chia seeds
flaxseeds
pepitas (pumpkin seeds)
pine nuts

poppy seeds
sesame seeds
sunflower seeds
almond slivers
tahini

BEANS

cannellini
lentils
black

pinto
navy
garbanzo

split peas
chickpeas

GRAINS, FLOURS AND BAKING

almond flour
amaranth
arrowroot flour
arrowroot powder
baking powder (gluten and
  additive free)
bicarbonate of soda (baking soda)
buckwheat groats, flour and pasta

brown rice and brown rice noodles
brown rice puffs
cacao butter
cacao powder
cacao nibs
coconut flakes
coconut flour
desiccated coconut

gluten-free self-raising flour
golden flaxmeal
millet
quinoa
vanilla extract (alcohol-free)
vanilla beans
white rice

FRESH HERBS AND SPICES

basil
cardamom
chives
cinnamon
coriander (cilantro)

cumin
dill
ginger
mint
nutmeg

oregano
parsley
sage
thyme
rosemary

CONDIMENTS AND SWEETENERS

Celtic sea salt
freshly ground black pepper
wheat-free tamari
apple cider vinegar
stevia drops
stevia powder

xylitol
coconut sugar
rice malt syrup
vegetable stock (sugar and
  additive-free)
tomato paste

coconut aminos
coconut nectar
dijon mustard
dulse flakes
brown rice crackers

MILKS AND DRINKS

nut milks
rice milk

coconut milk
soda water

FRUITS

apples
avocados
bananas

berries, fresh and frozen
lemons
oranges

pomegranate
pear
goji berry

MEAL PLANNER

Following a meal plan is a big motivator to keep you on track to nourishing yourself, and you can look forward to all of the delicious food options you have during the week. If you're cooking for one, you may consider making the full amount and freezing some to have at a later date.

Eating vegetables is my number-one form of health insurance. Make it yours too, and you will benefit enormously. We are all in this together.

	BREAKFAST	LUNCH	DINNER	DESSERT
MONDAY	Vegan Edible Smoothie (page 46) Zucchini Breakfast Muffin (page 64)	Mushroom with Red Quinoa Soup (page 99) Happy Kale Chips (page 190)	Nutritious Asian Bowl (page 126) Oriental Spinach (page 212)	Cauliflower and Raspberry Cheesecake (page 172)
TUESDAY	Warm Water with Lemon Green Pea Pancakes (page 69)	Lettuce Leaf Tacos (page 123)	Zesty Vegan Thai Soup (page 105)	Lemon Slices (page 174)
WEDNESDAY	Dandelion Tea with Almond Milk Indian-Spiced Vegetable Porridge (page 69)	Quinoa San Choy Bow (page 120)	Brown Lentil Chilli Bowl (page 129) Indian Whole Roasted Cauliflower (page 208)	Mixed Berry Cobbler (page 169)
THURSDAY	Warm Water with Lemon Vegan Omelette (page 61)	Creamy Summer Herb Soup (page 109) Cheesy Star Crackers (page 189)	Caramelised Onion Tart (page 138) A Side Order of Green Beans and Spinach (page 212)	Fresh Blueberry Fudge (page 166)
FRIDAY	Raw Superfood Greenie Smoothie (page 48)	Simple Vegan Caesar Salad (page 80) Decaf Almond Milk Latte	Lively Minted Pea Dip (page 198) with Muchos Nachos (page 125) Friday Night Pizza (page 141)	Spinach Ice Cream (page 181)
SATURDAY	Warm Water with Lemon Green Breakfast Bowl (page 66)	Black Bean Burgers with Green Salad (page 148)	Beautiful Beetroot Bourguignon (page 145) Savoury Smashed Root Vegetables (page 211)	Hazelnut, Chocolate and Berry Pudding (page 168)
SUNDAY	Mint Choc Chip Smoothie (page 51) Sunday Spinach Pikelets (page 71)	Kale, Strawberry and Avocado Salad with Poppy Seed Dressing (page 87) Sweet Spiced Nuts (page 203)	Lentil Moussaka (page 142) Celeriac Fries (page 186)	Triple Mint Slice (page 180)

DRINK YOUR VEGETABLES

Looking to clean up your dietary act, but not keen on gnawing your way through a kale salad first thing in the morning? Drinks don't have to taste like twigs and water – try one of these veggie-infused liquid meals, and fall in love with mornings all over again.

VEGAN EDIBLE SMOOTHIE

WF DF GF VEG VG   SERVES 1

There'll be no waking up on the wrong side of the bed with this magnificent meal-in-a-glass! Bursting with lively, activated nutrients and a beautiful, tangy and delicious berry zing, this smoothie is the perfect way to spruce up your morning.

185 ml (6 fl oz/3/4 cup) almond milk

30 g (1 oz/1/4 cup) raspberries

40 g (11/2 oz/1/4 cup) blueberries

35 g (11/4 oz/1/4 cup) strawberries, hulled

1 tablespoon freshly squeezed lemon juice

1 tablespoon organic almond butter
 (see note)

1 tablespoon flaxseeds

1 teaspoon alcohol-free vanilla extract

zest of 1 small lemon

pinch of stevia powder (optional)

Place all the ingredients in a glass jar and place in the fridge overnight. In the morning, pour the ingredients into a blender and process until completely smooth.

NOTE: If you don't have almond butter, substitute with 1 tablespoon raw almonds.

ᕀ Supercharged Tip ᕀ

If you're pressed for time and in a rush to get out the door in the mornings, make your smoothies the night before and place in a sealed jar in the fridge.

VEGETABLE RECOVERY JUICE

WF DF GF VEG VG   SERVES 2

The flavours in this refreshing recovery juice will raise a few brows, but only in the most positive way. Perfectly balanced, this is a textbook tonic for good health.

1 cucumber

1/4 purple cabbage

70 g (21/2 oz/1/2 cup) frozen blueberries

1/2 cup English spinach leaves

4 celery stalks

750 ml (26 fl oz/3 cups) coconut water

Place all the ingredients in a powerful blender, whizz and enjoy with a friend.

ᕀ Health Benefits ᕀ

Juicing helps your body better absorb the nutrients from vegetables, which will cleanse and nourish your cells.

RAW SUPERFOOD GREENIE SMOOTHIE

WF DF GF SF VEG VG SERVES 2

You'll be attracting only positive vibes with this smoothie that will wake you up from the inside out and leave you bursting with energy. Hailed as a mighty garden in a glass, this detoxifying blend is jam-packed with circulation-boosting chlorophyll. Guaranteed to put a swing in your step and a smile on your face.

1/2 cucumber, seeded

2 kale leaves, stems removed

3 celery stalks

2 cups English spinach leaves

1 tablespoon chia seeds

1/2 avocado, peeled and stone removed

1 teaspoon grated lemon zest

2 tablespoons freshly squeezed lemon juice

1 tablespoon coconut oil

375 ml (13 fl oz/1 1/2 cups) coconut water

Combine all the ingredients in a blender and whizz until you have the consistency you prefer. The coconut oil in this smoothie will help your body absorb the nutrients.

AKB (AVOCADO, KALE AND BANANA)

WF DF GF VEG VG   SERVES 1

If afternoon brain fog gets you down or you feel like you're dragging your feet through to Friday, the answer to mid-week, mid-morning delirium can be found in two powerful words: GREEN SMOOTHIE. This is creamy, dreamy and full of green goodness.

1 banana, peeled

250 ml (9 fl oz/1 cup) almond milk

2 kale leaves, stems removed

1/2 avocado, peeled and stone removed

Place all the ingredients in a blender and whizz until smooth.

VEGAN CHAI DANDY

WF DF GF VEG VG   SERVES 4

This might be mistaken for tasting like coffee but it's actually a great health-conscious alternative. The spices are enriched with health-promoting properties and it's as comforting as a hug.

1 tablespoon dried dandelion root
 (see note)

2 cinnamon sticks, broken into pieces

2/3 teaspoon whole cloves

5 cardamom pods, crushed

1 teaspoon whole black peppercorns

2.5 cm (1 inch) piece of ginger, thinly sliced

almond milk, to taste

1 tablespoon rice malt syrup, or 6 drops
 stevia liquid

Place the dandelion root, spices and ginger in a medium saucepan over high heat and add 1 litre (35 fl oz/4 cups) filtered water. Bring to the boil, then reduce the heat and simmer for 10 minutes.

Strain into a teapot and serve, adding almond milk and sweetener to taste.

NOTE: If you don't have dandelion roots, substitute the roots with two dandelion teabags.

MINT CHOC CHIP SMOOTHIE

WF   DF   GF   VEG   VG   SERVES 2

Move over mint slices (apart from the triple layered spinach one on page 180, of course)! This smoothie tastes just like mint choc chip ice cream, only it's much healthier. In fact, the traditional biscuity version has got nothing on this blended variety, which is full of sweet minty creaminess, minus the bloat.

1 peeled and frozen banana

1 bunch of English spinach leaves (see note)

1/4 cup organic nut butter

1/2 avocado, peeled and stone removed

handful of mint leaves, or 1/8 teaspoon
   alcohol-free peppermint extract

1 teaspoon alcohol-free vanilla extract

250 ml (9 fl oz/1 cup) almond milk

125 ml (4 fl oz/1/2 cup) coconut water

handful of ice (optional)

3 tablespoons raw cacao nibs

Place all the ingredients except the cacao nibs in a powerful blender and blend until smooth. Add the cacao nibs and blend for another 5–10 seconds. Pour into a tall glass and serve.

NOTE: You can substitute frozen spinach for the fresh.

IMMUNE-BOOSTING STRAWBERRY LASSI

●WF ♥GF ●VEG   MAKES 2 LARGE CUPS

Why not try this unique take on the lassi, a traditional Indian yoghurt-based drink commonly concocted with a combination of fruits and spices. This recipe opts for antioxidant-rich berries and the inflammation-busting wonder spice turmeric. It's a deliciously cooling and immune-boosting breakfast or anytime-of-the-day solution.

To veganise: Replace the yoghurt with 250 ml (9 fl oz/1 cup) coconut milk and 250 ml (9 fl oz/1 cup) coconut water.

520 g (1 lb 2½ oz/2 cups) plain, sugar-free Greek or sheep's yoghurt

150 g (5½ oz/1 cup) strawberries, hulled (see note)

2 teaspoons freshly grated ginger

juice of ½ lemon

1 teaspoon alcohol-free vanilla extract

1 tablespoon ground turmeric

4–5 ice cubes

Place all the ingredients in a blender and whizz until smooth.

NOTE: If strawberries aren't in season, simply substitute with the same quantity of frozen strawberries, or other berries of your choice.

PUMPKIN AND TURMERIC SMOOTHIE

WF DF GF SF VEG VG   MAKES 1 LARGE OR 2 SMALL

Who would've thought this golden garden dweller could make a scrumptious smoothie addition? In this delicious smoothie, pumpkin waves goodbye to the soup pot and the Sunday roast, taking centre stage in your blender.

375 ml (13 fl oz/1 1/2 cups) coconut water

1/2 avocado, peeled and stone removed

125 g (4 1/2 oz/1/2 cup) cooked pumpkin (winter squash)

1 teaspoon grated orange zest

1 teaspoon turmeric

1/2 teaspoon grated ginger

1/4 teaspoon stevia powder, to sweeten

Place all the ingredients in a high-speed blender and blend for around 30–45 seconds until smooth.

Health Benefits

Turmeric is a lively root, with a heady, earthy fragrance, known for its Hogwarts'-quality magical healing powers. It can transform unglamorous, frumpy vegetables and smoothies into golden, anti-inflammatory bundles of wellness.

STRAWBERRY GRANITA

WF · DF · GF · VEG · VG   SERVES 2

Ready for a transcendental experience? As your granita starts to melt, it becomes slushy and the texture, coupled with the flavour of the berries, is out of this world.

3 punnets of frozen strawberries, hulled

1 tablespoon rice malt syrup, or sweetener of your choice

2 tablespoons additive-free coconut milk

unsweetened coconut flakes, to serve

Place the frozen strawberries in a blender with the rice malt syrup or sweetener. Blend until smooth, and then transfer to a freezer-proof dish and place in the freezer until the top layer starts to freeze.

Remove from the freezer, return to the blender and blend again to icy flakes.

Divide the coconut milk between two glasses, add the granita, top with the coconut flakes and serve.

RASPBERRY SPRITZER

WF · DF · GF · VEG · VG   SERVES 2

To think that only fizzy drink corporations can create a bottom-kicking beverage is the misconception of the century. The proof is in this delicious sparkling juice, guaranteed to dazzle drinkers with its bright pink hue and zinging flavours of raspberry and coconut. Place it on the summer lunch table and wow your friends and guests.

125 g (4^{1}/$_{2}$ oz/1 cup) frozen raspberries

125 ml (4 fl oz/^{1}/$_{2}$ cup) freshly squeezed lemon juice

^{1}/$_{4}$ teaspoon stevia liquid, or sweetener of your choice

500 ml (17 fl oz/2 cups) sparkling water

6 coconut water ice cubes

Place the raspberries in a bowl and squash them with a fork. Set aside for 15 minutes. Transfer the raspberries to a fine mesh sieve, set over a jug. Add the lemon juice, then use the back of a spoon to push the raspberries through the sieve, scraping the outside of the sieve as you go.

Add the stevia and stir well. Add the sparkling water and ice and stir again.

Divide between two glasses and serve with a straw. If the raspberry settles at the bottom of your glass, give it a stir.

BREAKFAST

When you're looking to hike up your six a day, it makes logical sense to involve vegetables in every meal. Reap the benefits of an amazingly nutritious breakfast with a Green Breakfast Bowl, let your mind wander to exotic destinations with an Indian-Spiced Vegetable Porridge, or give peas a chance with Green Pea Pancakes.

AMARANTH, WALNUT AND PUMPKIN PORRIDGE

●WF ●DF ●GF ●VEG ●VG   SERVES 2

This earthy porridge is the perfect morning comfort food. It's super steamy and deliciously creamy. Delectability aside, this breakfast also boasts a healing hit of medicinal anti-inflammatory spices.

1/4 **pumpkin (winter squash), peeled and chopped into 3 cm (1 1/4 inch) pieces**

115 g (4 oz/1 cup) **walnuts**

100 g (3 1/2 oz/1/2 cup) **amaranth, soaked in water overnight, see note**

375 ml (13 fl oz/1 1/2 cups) **coconut or almond milk, plus extra, to serve**

pinch of Celtic sea salt

1/2 teaspoon **ground cinnamon**

1/2 teaspoon **nutmeg**

1/4 teaspoon **ground ginger**

1/2 teaspoon **alcohol-free vanilla extract**

1 teaspoon **grated lemon zest**

1 tablespoon **rice malt syrup to sweeten (optional)**

20 g (3/4 oz/1/3 cup) **unsweetened coconut flakes**

Line a bamboo steamer with baking paper and steam the pumpkin over a saucepan of gently simmering water for 7 minutes. Transfer to a food processor and purée.

Dry roast the walnuts in a frying pan over medium heat and set aside.

Drain the amaranth in a fine sieve and rinse under cold running water. Transfer to a saucepan with the coconut milk, pumpkin purée, salt, spices, vanilla and lemon zest and bring to the boil. Reduce the temperature to its lowest setting, cover and simmer, stirring often, for 15 minutes. You may need to add more coconut milk if the mixture is looking too dry. Remove from the heat and let it rest for 10 minutes.

To serve, divide between two bowls, drizzle with the extra coconut milk and rice malt syrup, if using, and scatter over the walnuts and coconut flakes.

NOTE: You can substitute the same quantity of rolled oats for the amaranth.

SWEET POTATO, LEEK AND THYME BAKE

WF · DF · GF · SF · VEG · VG   SERVES 4 AS A MAIN, OR 6 AS A SIDE

It's a shame that some find breakfast so limited in its expressions. Expand your horizons with this veggie-filled, oven-baked delight. The coconut milk in this dish really transforms a handful of simple ingredients into a wonderfully creamy bake which can hold its own equally well on the lunch table.

1 tablespoon cold-pressed extra virgin olive oil, plus extra, for greasing

1 leek, white part only, trimmed, washed and cut into half moons

1 garlic clove, peeled and sliced

500 ml (17 fl oz/2 cups) additive-free coconut milk

2 thyme sprigs

1/4 teaspoon nutmeg

1/4 teaspoon ground cinnamon

500 g (1 lb 2 oz) frozen spinach, thawed

2 sweet potatoes, peeled and thinly sliced

3 tablespoons nutritional yeast flakes

Preheat the oven to 180°C (350°F/Gas 4) and grease an 18 cm (7 inch) ovenproof dish.

Heat the oil in a saucepan over medium heat and sauté the leek and garlic for 5 minutes, or until brown. Add the coconut milk, thyme, nutmeg and cinnamon and heat slowly. Just before it comes to the boil, remove from the heat and set aside.

Squeeze all the excess water from the spinach.

Place alternate layers of sweet potato and spinach into the ovenproof dish, adding the coconut mixture when you are halfway – ideally you will have three layers each of sweet potato and spinach. Finish with a layer of sweet potato and sprinkle over the nutritional yeast flakes.

Transfer to the oven and bake for 55 minutes or until golden and the sweet potato is cooked through.

VEGAN OMELETTE

WF   DF   GF   SF   VEG   VG   SERVES 2

If eggs make you scramble, then whip up this vegan omelette. Top with your choice of fillings and breakfast just got a million times easier.

60 g (2¹/4 oz/¹/2 cup) superfine besan (chickpea flour)

2 tablespoons nutritional yeast flakes

1 tablespoon ground flaxseeds or chia seeds

¹/2 teaspoon turmeric

1 teaspoon dried Italian herbs

¹/2 teaspoon gluten-free baking powder

Celtic sea salt and freshly ground black pepper, to taste

1 tablespoon extra virgin coconut oil

1 garlic clove, peeled and crushed

1 handful of English spinach leaves

1 tomato, chopped

Mix the besan, nutritional yeast flakes, flaxseeds, turmeric, herbs, baking powder and salt and pepper together in a bowl with 185 ml (6 fl oz/3/4 cup) of filtered water. Stir well and set aside for 10 minutes to thicken. The mixture should be able to be poured – if not, add more water.

Add the coconut oil to a small frying pan over medium heat. Sauté half the garlic for a few minutes and then add half the batter to the middle of the pan. Use the back of a spoon to smooth the mixture evenly over the pan. Add half the spinach and half the tomato and cook for 5–6 minutes, or until small bubbles appear on the surface. Carefully fold the omelette over into a cigar shape and transfer to a plate to keep warm while you cook the other omelette.

Repeat with the remaining ingredients and serve.

CHAI CHIA BREAKFAST PUDDING

WF DF GF SF VEG VG   SERVES 4

Stuck for a breakfast idea that will switch on your senses and entice a happy morning mood? This chai chia breakfast pudding will do just the trick. Full of antioxidants, vitamins, essential fatty acids and an exotic blend of chai spices, this pudding will fill you with joy.

1/4 teaspoon Celtic sea salt

40 g (1 1/2 oz/1/4 cup) hazelnuts

120 g (4 1/4 oz/3/4 cup) raw cashews

1/2 teaspoon alcohol-free vanilla extract

6 drops stevia liquid, or 2 tablespoons sweetener of your choice, such as xylitol or rice malt syrup

1/2 teaspoon cardamom

1/2 teaspoon nutmeg

1/2 teaspoon ground cinnamon

30 g (1 oz/1/4 cup) chia seeds

1/2 cup chopped nuts, to serve

strawberries, to serve (optional)

almond milk, to serve

Combine the salt, hazelnuts, cashews, vanilla, stevia and spices with 750 ml (26 fl oz/3 cups) of filtered water in a blender and whizz until smooth.

Transfer to a bowl and add the chia seeds. Stir to combine well, then cover and place in the fridge overnight.

To serve, scatter with chopped nuts and strawberries, if using, and add almond milk.

Health Benefits

Chia seeds are teeny tiny, but impressively clever. When soaked in water they transform into a highly detoxifying gel. They absorb other flavours well.

ZUCCHINI BREAKFAST MUFFINS

●WF ●GF ●SF ●VEG   MAKES 6 LARGE OR 12 SMALL MUFFINS

These nourishing morsels will give any sugar-laden muffin a run for its money. They taste so delicious you would never suspect that they are loaded with veggie goodness.

To veganise: Substitute the eggs with 2 tablespoons ground or whole chia or flaxseeds soaked in 120 ml (3¾ fl oz) of water for 15 minutes, and the butter with 3 tablespoons light olive oil.

150 g (5½ oz/1½ cups) almond meal or
   gluten-free flour

60 g (2¼ oz/½ cup) toasted walnuts

1 teaspoon bicarbonate of soda
   (baking soda)

½ teaspoon gluten-free baking powder

¼ teaspoon Celtic sea salt

1 teaspoon ground cinnamon

½ teaspoon nutmeg

¾ teaspoon stevia powder

205 g (7¼ oz/1½ cups) grated
   zucchini (courgette)

2 organic eggs, beaten

80 ml (2½ fl oz/⅓ cup) additive-free
   coconut milk

¼ cup melted organic butter

Preheat the oven to 180°C (350°F/Gas 4) and place paper liners in a 6-hole (250 ml/9 fl oz/1 cup) or 12-hole (80 ml/2½ fl oz/⅓ cup) muffin tin.

Place all the dry ingredients in a bowl and mix well to combine.

Squeeze the zucchini to remove any excess moisture.

In a separate bowl, whisk the eggs, coconut milk and butter together. Fold into the dry ingredients and add the zucchini.

Divide the mixture among the prepared muffin holes and bake in the oven for 45 minutes, or until golden brown.

Place onto a wire rack to cool.

These will keep for 4 days in a sealed container.

SPINACH AND CARROT MUFFINS

● WF ● GF ● SF ● VEG   MAKES 6 LARGE OR 12 SMALL MUFFINS

Getting your daily dose of greens has never been more delicious. Packed with nutrient-dense spinach, these muffins are a delicious way to enjoy a hearty portion of vegetables with every bite.
To veganise: Substitute the eggs with 3 tablespoons ground or whole chia or flaxseeds soaked in 125 ml (4 fl oz/1/2 cup) of water for 15 minutes, and the yoghurt with 125 ml (4 fl oz/1/2 cup) of coconut milk.

40 g (1 1/2 oz/1/3 cup) tapioca flour

130 g (4 1/2 oz/1 cup) buckwheat flour

1 teaspoon gluten-free baking powder

3 tablespoons flaxseeds

pinch of Celtic sea salt and freshly ground black pepper

1/2 teaspoon nutmeg

3 organic eggs, beaten

260 g (9 1/4 oz/1 cup) full-fat yoghurt

2 carrots, coarsely grated

1 bunch of English spinach leaves, roughly chopped

1 small brown onion, finely chopped

juice and zest of 1 lemon

1 garlic clove, minced

40 g (1 1/2 oz/1/4 cup) pepitas (pumpkin seeds) (optional)

Preheat the oven to 170°C (325°F/Gas 3) and place paper liners in a 6-hole (250 ml/9 fl oz/1 cup) or 12-hole (80 ml/2 1/2 fl oz/1/3 cup) muffin tin.

Mix the two flours, baking powder, flaxseeds, salt and pepper and nutmeg in a bowl and set aside.

In a separate bowl, place the eggs and yoghurt and stir to combine. Add the carrot, spinach, onion, lemon juice and zest and garlic and stir until well combined.

Add the dry ingredients to the veggie mixture and stir well with a spatula. Pour the batter into the muffin holes and top with pepitas, if using.

Bake in the oven for 20–25 minutes, or until a toothpick comes out clean. Remove from the oven and transfer to a wire rack to cool.

These will keep for 4 days in a sealed container.

GREEN BREAKFAST BOWL

WF   GF   SF   VEG   SERVES 3

Green veggies are the perfect energy booster and are incredibly dense in nutrients. This delicious green breakfast bowl will propel you miles ahead of sugary, boxed breakfast-cereal eaters.

To veganise: Swap the eggs for 2 tablespoons nutritional yeast flakes, and the butter for extra virgin olive oil.

200 g (7 oz/1 cup) quinoa

1 cup chopped kale

1 tablespoon organic butter, for frying

3 organic eggs

60 g (2¼ oz/¼ cup) basil pesto (see page 194)

1 avocado, peeled, stone removed and cut into wedges

juice of ½ lemon

Celtic sea salt and freshly ground black pepper

Cook the quinoa according to the packet directions.

Line a bamboo steamer with baking paper and steam the kale over a saucepan of gently simmering water for 10 minutes, or until tender. Set aside.

Meanwhile, add the butter to a frying pan over medium heat and fry the eggs until done to your liking.

To serve, divide the quinoa, kale and pesto between three bowls. Top with a fried egg, place the avocado on the side and finish with a squeeze of lemon for extra zing. Season to taste.

GREEN PEA PANCAKES

WF GF SF VEG   MAKES 10 SMALL OR 6 LARGE PANCAKES

To veganise this recipe, substitute the eggs with 135 g (4³/4 oz/¹/2 cup) apple sauce, and the goat's cheese with 1 tablespoon of yeast flakes and 60 ml (2 fl oz/¹/4 cup) coconut milk.

215 g (7¹/2 oz/1¹/2 cups) frozen green peas, thawed

1 teaspoon freshly grated ginger

2 tablespoons freshly chopped parsley

2 organic eggs

zest of 1 lemon

1 tablespoon wheat-free tamari

2 tablespoons coconut flour

150 g (5¹/2 oz) goat's cheese

Celtic sea salt and freshly ground black pepper

extra virgin coconut oil, for frying

lemon cheeks, to serve

Place the peas in a large bowl and mash with a fork. Add the ginger, parsley, eggs, lemon zest, tamari, coconut flour and goat's cheese. Season with salt and pepper.

Heat the coconut oil in a large frying pan over low heat. Making several pancakes at a time, spoon the batter into the pan in 60 ml (2 fl oz/¹/4 cup) quantities. Cook for about 5 minutes, or until the batter has set and is bubbling, then carefully flip the pancakes and cook on the other side for a minute or two, or until browned to your liking.

Remove from the pan and keep warm while you cook the rest. Repeat with the remaining coconut oil and batter until all the batter is cooked.

Serve with lemon cheeks. If you would like to serve them for lunch, add some leafy greens or steamed vegetables.

INDIAN-SPICED VEGETABLE PORRIDGE

WF DF GF SF VEG VG   SERVES 2

1 bunch of English spinach leaves

¹/2 cup grated zucchini (courgette)

¹/2 cup grated carrot

¹/2 teaspoon ground cinnamon

2 whole cloves

¹/4 teaspoon nutmeg

¹/2 teaspoon ground ginger

1 teaspoon grated lemon zest (optional)

¹/4 teaspoon stevia powder

250 ml (9 fl oz/1 cup) coconut milk

80 g (2³/4 oz/¹/2 cup) chopped almonds

pinch of Celtic sea salt

30 g (1 oz/¹/4 cup) chopped almonds, to serve

Cut the English spinach leaves into small strips and add to a small saucepan with the zucchini, carrot, spices, zest, if using, stevia and coconut milk and bring to the boil. Add the almonds and salt and lower the heat. Simmer for 5 minutes.

Serve topped with the almonds.

QUINOA PANCAKES

● WF ● DF ● GF ● SF ● VEG   MAKES 12

Quinoa really is the ultimate breakfast food. Containing all nine essential amino acids, this gluten-free seed is a complete protein that will fill you up without the bloat. Quinoa absorbs flavours beautifully, so it makes an incredible pancake.

To veganise: Substitute the eggs with 270 g (9½ oz/1 cup) apple sauce or 1 banana, and use coconut oil to fry.

810 g (1 lb 12 oz/3 cups) cooked quinoa

185 ml (6 fl oz/¾ cup) almond milk

4 organic eggs

3 teaspoons gluten-free baking powder

pinch of Celtic sea salt

extra virgin coconut oil or organic butter, for frying

stevia powder, for serving

lemon wedges, for serving

Place all the ingredients, except the coconut oil, stevia powder and lemon wedges, in a food processor and blend until smooth. If the mixture seems too thick, add more milk.

Heat the oil or butter in a large frying pan. Making several pancakes at a time, spoon the batter into the pan in 1 tablespoon quantities. Cook over medium heat for 5 minutes until the pancakes start to bubble on top. Carefully flip the pancakes over and continue cooking for 5 minutes, or until they are golden brown.

Remove from the pan and keep warm while you cook the remaining batter. Repeat until all the batter is cooked.

Serve warm, sprinkled with stevia and with lemon wedges on the side.

NOTE: You can make savoury versions by adding nutritional yeast flakes and serving with a green salad.

⚜ Health Benefits ⚜

Quinoa keeps your blood sugar levels in check. It's a whole grain with the germ, endosperm and bran intact, bringing a host of nutrients and healthy fats to the mix.

SUNDAY SPINACH PIKELETS

WF   DF   GF   SF   VEG   MAKES 8

Perfect for a lazy Sunday morning lolling on the couch with your favourite novel, you'll love these fluffy pikelets.

To veganise: Substitute the eggs with 2 tablespoons ground or whole chia or flaxseeds soaked in 120 ml (3¾ fl oz) of water for 15 minutes.

1 bunch of English spinach leaves

30 g (1 oz/⅓ cup) chia seeds

50 g (1¾ oz/½ cup) almond meal

2 organic eggs

1 tablespoon organic nut butter

1 teaspoon ground cinnamon

170 ml (5½ fl oz/⅔ cup) almond milk

good pinch of Celtic sea salt

1 tablespoon extra virgin coconut oil,
   for frying

Place all the ingredients, except the coconut oil, in a food processor and mix until smooth. Set aside for 10 minutes.

Heat half the coconut oil in a large frying pan over medium heat. Making several pikelets at a time, spoon the batter into the pan in 2 tablespoon (40 ml/1¼ fl oz) quantities. Cook for about 5 minutes, then carefully flip the pikelets and cook them on the other side for a minute or two.

Remove from the pan and keep warm while you cook the rest. Repeat with the remaining coconut oil and batter until all the pikelets are cooked.

These are delicious served with Cashew Sour Cream (see page 217) or Cashew Nut Yoghurt (see page 219).

MINI CHIVE PANCAKES

●WF ●DF ●GF ●SF ●VEG   MAKES 10

High-five these mini chive discs of yumminess. I have a feeling they'll be in the running as a new breakfast favourite, because they're simply a joy to whip up and eat. Enjoy them for breakfast or as an afternoon tea treat.

To veganise: Substitute the eggs with 6 tablespoons ground or whole chia or flaxseeds soaked in 250 ml (9 fl oz/1 cup) of water for 15 minutes.

240 g (8³/4 oz/1¹/2 cups) brown rice flour

¹/2 teaspoon Celtic sea salt

2 tablespoons toasted sesame seeds

125 ml (4 fl oz/¹/2 cup) additive-free coconut milk

1 teaspoon wheat-free tamari

1 garlic clove, peeled and crushed

6 large organic eggs

20 g (³/4 oz/¹/3 cup) finely chopped chives

1 tablespoon extra virgin coconut oil

lemon wedges, to serve

Place the flour, salt and sesame seeds in a large bowl and mix to combine.

In a separate bowl, whisk the coconut milk, tamari, garlic, eggs and chives together with 250 ml (9 fl oz/1 cup) of water. Pour into the bowl with the dry ingredients and mix until smooth. You may need to add a little more water. Let the batter sit for 10 minutes.

Heat the oil in a small frying pan and add about 60 ml (2 fl oz/¹/4 cup) of the batter. Swirl so the base of the pan is covered and cook for 5 minutes, or until the base is brown. Flip and cook on the other side until set.

Transfer to a plate to keep warm while you repeat with the remaining batter.

Serve with the lemon wedges.

⊱ Supercharged Tip ⊰

Make these pancakes the day before, then reheat for 10 minutes in a very low oven for a light breakfast on the go.

SAVOURY ZUCCHINI FRITTERS

WF DF GF SF VEG   MAKES 10

I like to double park these alongside a generous serving of Happy Kale Chips (see page 190) to really get my green on at breakfast time. They're easily digestible so you'll sail effortlessly through to lunch without a hint of the hungries.

To veganise: Substitute the eggs with 3 tablespoons ground or whole chia or flaxseeds soaked in 160 ml (5¼ fl oz) of water for 15 minutes.

3 zucchini (courgettes)

¼ cup very finely chopped cauliflower

1 bunch of English spinach leaves, finely chopped (see note)

½ onion, finely chopped

1 garlic clove, peeled and crushed

1 tablespoon parsley, chopped

1 tablespoon mint, chopped

good pinch of Celtic sea salt

freshly ground black pepper

zest of 1 lemon

3 organic eggs, lightly beaten

50 g (1¾ oz/½ cup) almond meal

1 tablespoon extra virgin coconut oil

Grate the zucchini and place in a colander with a pinch of salt. Let it sit for 10 minutes to remove the excess moisture.

Place the zucchini in a large bowl with the rest of the ingredients except the coconut oil. Mix well – the mixture should hold together.

Add the coconut oil to a large frying pan over medium heat. Cooking several fritters at a time, spoon the batter into the pan in 2 tablespoon quantities. Cook for 3 minutes on each side, or until golden.

Remove from the pan, transfer to a plate to keep warm and repeat with the remaining batter until all the fritters are cooked.

NOTE: You could substitute the English spinach with 1 cup thawed frozen spinach.

SALADS AND SOUPS

Say goodbye to bloat-inducing, sodium-laden soup from a tin: instead, cuddle up with these simple, irresistible broths that are bursting with nutrients. On the fresh and crunchy front, my Kale, Strawberry and Avocado Salad with Poppy Seed Dressing, or Eggplant, Pomegranate and Minted Quinoa will get you out of your salad rut. Take advantage of seasonal produce, earthy spices and high-impact flavours, and be bowled over by these made-from-scratch dishes of virtuousness.

HOW TO BUILD A HEALTHY SALAD

Salad chains need to get back in their boxes. It's just as affordable and easy to design your own using the freshest, most nutritious ingredients, minus the sugar- and salt-laden dressings. Work more vegetables into your life and drizzle them with smart fats. Get out of your salad rut with a Kale, Strawberry and Avocado with Poppy Seed Dressing sensation, go simple with a Vegan Caesar or dig your fork into an Eggplant, Pomegranate and Minted Quinoa masterpiece. Building a healthy salad is a snap.

- Firstly choose a base such as mixed leafy greens, baby spinach, kale or rocket (arugula).
- Add crunch with essential nutrients like beans, cauliflower, carrot, celery, cucumber, radish, sprouts or onion.
- Next add a good quality protein such as quinoa, buckwheat, eggs or chickpeas.
- Drop in some good fats like avocado, flaxseed oil, olive oil or tahini.
- Sprinkle on some nuts or seeds.
- Green it up further by adding flavoursome herbs such as mint, basil, coriander (cilantro) or parsley. Toss and enjoy.

OVER THE RAINBOW SALAD WITH TAHINI AND LEMON DRESSING

◆ WF　● DF　● GF　● SF　● VEG　● VG　　　SERVES 2

For a healthy spin, combine any raw veggies in this kaleidoscopic feast for a completely balanced meal. It's easy to throw together and deliciously healthy. The tahini and lemon dressing tastes so much better than any pre-packaged dressing you would buy in the grocery store, and it takes a nanosecond to prepare.

2 cups mixed salad greens

1 red onion, sliced

1 small beetroot (beet), thinly sliced or spiralised

40 g (1 1/2 oz/1/2 cup) shredded purple cabbage

1 red capsicum (pepper), seeds and membrane removed and diced

1 yellow capsicum (pepper), seeds and membrane removed and diced

1 carrot, thinly sliced or spiralised

1 cucumber, diced

1 avocado, peeled, stone removed and sliced into wedges

sprinkle of pepitas (pumpkin seeds)

handful of bean sprouts

1 tablespoon sesame seeds, to garnish

TAHINI AND LEMON DRESSING

135 g (4 3/4 oz/1/2 cup) tahini

1 tablespoon freshly squeezed lemon juice

5 drops stevia liquid

1 teaspoon Celtic sea salt, or to taste

Place all the salad ingredients, except the sesame seeds, in a bowl and carefully mix together.

To make the dressing, place all the ingredients in a bowl with 60 ml (2 fl oz/1/4 cup) of filtered water and blend until a smooth paste forms. Add more filtered water, if required.

Dress the salad, sprinkle over the sesame seeds and serve immediately.

⸕ Supercharged Tip ⸕

For a cheesier dressing, add 2 tablespoons of nutritional yeast flakes. If you love soy, this salad can be garnished with cubed fresh, organic tofu, marinated in wheat-free tamari for 5 minutes and fried in a small amount of coconut oil on all sides until crispy.

SIMPLE VEGAN CAESAR SALAD

● WF ● DF ● GF ● SF ● VEG ● VG   SERVES 4

If you haven't already, you'll happily farewell bacon and eggs once you've had a taste of this show-up Caesar salad. Fried tempeh with tamari gives the exact hit of saltiness needed to boost the flavour in this vegan-friendly twist on the original.

60 ml (2 fl oz/$1/4$ cup) cold-pressed extra virgin olive oil

300 g (10$1/2$ oz) block of tempeh, chopped into 5 mm ($1/4$ inch) cubes

60 ml (2 fl oz/$1/4$ cup) wheat-free tamari

1 cos (romaine) lettuce, washed, dried and torn

1 small bunch of spring onions (scallions), roughly chopped

DRESSING

3 tablespoons organic almond butter

2 small garlic cloves, finely chopped

3 tablespoons nutritional yeast flakes

2 tablespoons wheat-free tamari

60 ml (2 fl oz/$1/4$ cup) freshly squeezed lemon juice

3 tablespoons sugar-free dijon mustard

2 tablespoons flaxseed oil

freshly ground black pepper

Heat the olive oil in a frying pan over medium heat and fry the tempeh for 5–7 minutes, or until golden. Add the tamari and heat until warm. Remove from the heat and set aside to cool.

To make the dressing, mix all the ingredients in a bowl with 60 ml (2 fl oz/$1/4$ cup) of filtered water.

Place the lettuce and spring onions in a bowl and spoon over the dressing, tossing to ensure the salad is evenly coated. Sprinkle the cooled tempeh over the top and serve.

GREEN BEAN SALAD WITH LEMONY DRESSING

WF DF GF SF VEG VG   SERVES 4

We've all experienced a questionable serving of green beans at some stage in our lives; the boiled-to-death, soggy, grey-tinged version. These are the food experiences that turn people into veggie enemies. It pains me to think that the green bean isn't always able to display its true splendour, but when given the respect it deserves, the humble green bean accompaniment can drop the jaws of an entire celebrity chef panel. This dish does just that with its zingy flavour and unquestionable crunch.

375 g (13 oz/3 cups) topped and tailed green beans

1 spring onion (scallion), chopped

3 tablespoons sugar-free mustard

6 drops stevia liquid

2 tablespoons freshly squeezed lemon juice

1 tablespoon apple cider vinegar

60 ml (2 fl oz/¼ cup) cold-pressed extra virgin olive oil

Celtic sea salt and freshly ground black pepper

50 g (1¾ oz/½ cup) flaked almonds

Line a bamboo steamer with baking paper and steam the beans over a saucepan of gently simmering water for 2 minutes. Refresh in iced water and pat dry with a clean tea towel (dish towel).

Place the beans in a bowl with the spring onion and set aside.

Whisk the mustard, stevia, lemon juice, apple cider vinegar and olive oil together until combined and season to taste.

Pour the dressing over the beans and spring onions, top with the flaked almonds and serve.

CURRIED EGG AND WALNUT SALAD

●WF ●GF ●SF ●VEG   SERVES 4

A creative take on your grandmother's classic curried eggs, this filling salad is the perfect light lunch solution. Eggs really do have everything going for them: artfully packaged by nature, and meticulously balanced in protein, good fats and carbohydrates. They're a faultless workday fuel.
To veganise: Substitute the eggs with a cubed avocado, and the yoghurt with coconut milk.

8 asparagus spears

1 tablespoon cold-pressed extra virgin olive oil

juice of 1/2 lemon

6 organic eggs

4 bunches of broccolini, roughly chopped

60 g (2 1/4 oz/1/2 cup) walnuts

150 g (5 1/2 oz/1 cup) cherry tomatoes

DRESSING

130 g (4 1/2 oz/1/2 cup) full-fat Greek or sheep's yoghurt

2 teaspoons curry powder

pinch of cayenne pepper

pinch of Celtic sea salt

freshly ground black pepper, to taste

Preheat the oven to 200°C (400°F/Gas 6).

Snap the woody ends off the asparagus, lay the spears in a single layer on a baking tray and drizzle with the olive oil. Roll the spears in the olive oil to ensure they are evenly coated.

Bake for 8–10 minutes, or until lightly browned and tender when pierced with a fork. Drizzle with a little lemon juice and set aside.

Bring a saucepan of water to the boil, place the eggs in the water, lower the heat to medium and boil for 7–8 minutes. Remove from the saucepan and set aside to cool before peeling.

Meanwhile, line a bamboo steamer with baking paper and steam the broccolini for 5–7 minutes, or until *al dente*.

Toast the walnuts in a dry pan for a couple of minutes on each side. Remove from the pan and set aside to cool.

Whisk all the dressing ingredients together in a small bowl.

Halve the eggs, then divide between four plates with the remaining ingredients. Drizzle over the dressing and serve.

SHAVED BRUSSELS, FENNEL AND KALE SALAD

WF   DF   GF   SF   VEG   VG   SERVES 4

Green veggies cover a multitude of sins. They really are the most important food for disease prevention, detoxification and all-round vibrant health. Utilising some of the less popular greens, all this salad requires of you is a little fine slicing and a quick, crafty dressing to make them mouthwateringly good.

8–10 Brussels sprouts, trimmed and shaved

1 small fennel bulb, trimmed and thinly sliced

1 bunch of kale, stems removed, leaves torn into bite-sized pieces, washed and spun dry

1 cup baby rocket (arugula)

1/2 red onion, thinly sliced

55 g (2 oz/1/3 cup) almonds with skins, toasted

1 tablespoon nutritional yeast flakes, to serve

DRESSING

60 ml (2 fl oz/1/4 cup) cold-pressed extra virgin olive oil

2 teaspoons freshly squeezed lemon juice

1 tablespoon apple cider vinegar

1 tablespoon sugar-free mustard

1/2 teaspoon Celtic sea salt

Combine all the salad ingredients, except the yeast flakes, in a large bowl.

Whisk the dressing ingredients together and pour over the salad. Toss to coat well and sprinkle with the nutritional yeast flakes.

QUINOA, PEAR, ZUCCHINI AND RED ONION SALAD

WF DF GF VEG VG   SERVES 4

If you're in need of a healthy, easy-to-make and satisfying salad, then look no further. Pulling lunch together will only take moments if you have leftover quinoa in the fridge. You can experiment with seasonal ingredients and add your favourite vegetables, such as cooked cauliflower, kale or squash.

270 g (9^1/2 oz/1 cup) cooked quinoa

1 large zucchini (courgette), sliced

1 pear, thinly sliced

1 red onion, chopped

^{1}/2 cup basil leaves, chopped

DRESSING

2–3 garlic cloves, minced

125 ml (4 fl oz/^{1}/2 cup) freshly squeezed lemon juice

2 tablespoons cold-pressed extra virgin olive oil

1 tablespoon Celtic sea salt

Place the cooked quinoa in a serving bowl. Add the zucchini, pear, onion and basil.

To make the dressing, mix all the ingredients together.

Fold the dressing into the quinoa salad and toss to ensure it's evenly coated.

Serve and enjoy.

Health Benefits

Quinoa has high levels of amino acids and protein, and is a good source of iron, calcium and potassium – food values no grain can rival. It provides your body with copper, zinc, magnesium and folate, vitamin B6, thiamine, niacin and riboflavin. The riboflavin present in quinoa reduces the frequency of migraine attacks by relaxing the blood vessels, reducing constriction and easing tension.

KALE, STRAWBERRY AND AVOCADO SALAD WITH POPPY SEED DRESSING

● WF   ● DF   ● GF   ● VEG   ● VG   SERVES 2–3

This salad is full of good-for-you vegetables and berries, and topped with healthy fats, which combine to make a nutrient-dense meal suitable for all. It's a beautiful blend of sweetness and bitterness, and the vibrant assortment of colours makes you want to dive straight in. Just one serving of kale delivers protein, fibre and impressive doses of vitamins A and C, making it rich in powerful antioxidants. It's a welcome dish to bring to summer lunches where many dishes are typically full of carbohydrates and, if you're looking for a knockout marinade, this dressing is multi-dimensional!

juice of 1 lemon

2 tablespoons cold-pressed extra virgin olive oil

1 bunch of kale, stems removed, leaves chopped into thin slices

pinch of Celtic sea salt

1 avocado, peeled, stone removed and sliced into wedges

40 g (1 1/2 oz/1/4 cup) pine nuts

150 g (5 1/2 oz/1 cup) strawberries, hulled and quartered

POPPY SEED DRESSING

60 ml (2 fl oz/1/4 cup) cold-pressed extra virgin olive oil

2 tablespoons apple cider vinegar

1 teaspoon sugar-free mustard

1/2 shallot, diced

1 tablespoon poppy seeds

pinch of Celtic sea salt

1 tablespoon wheat-free tamari

Combine the lemon juice and olive oil and then massage it into the kale leaves with a pinch of salt. Continue rubbing the mixture into the leaves until they soften.

Add the kale to a salad bowl with the avocado, pine nuts and strawberries.

To make the dressing, whisk all the ingredients together.

Serve the salad topped with the poppy seed dressing.

 Supercharged Tip

This salad can be stored in the fridge in an airtight container for 4 days.

WARM BEETROOT, CARROT AND PEAR SALAD

🍎 WF 🔲 DF 🍐 GF 🔶 VEG 🔷 VG   SERVES 4

The trusty roasting tray is legendary in its ability to intensify and caramelise the naturally sweet flavours in vegetables. Beetroot and carrot are two veggies that are especially enriched in flavour and texture when given a little love in the oven.

1 small bunch of carrots, chopped

6–8 baby beetroot (beets), peeled and cubed

2 tablespoons mixed dried herbs, such as
coriander (cilantro), fenugreek, cumin
and star anise

2 tablespoons apple cider vinegar

big splash of orange-infused almond oil

Celtic sea salt and freshly ground
black pepper

150 g (5½ oz/1 cup) cherry
tomatoes, chopped

1 pear, thinly sliced

large handful of parsley leaves, chopped

2 tablespoons sesame seeds

Preheat the oven to 200°C (400°F/Gas 6).

Place the carrot and beetroot in a baking tray and add the herbs, apple cider vinegar, almond oil and salt and pepper. Mix so the vegetables are evenly coated.

Place in the oven and bake for 45 minutes, turning the veggies after 20 minutes.

Remove from the oven and set aside to cool.

Meanwhile, add the tomatoes and pear to a serving bowl. Add the cooled vegetables with the cooking juices, then add the parsley and sesame seeds and enjoy.

Health Benefits

A superstar ingredient, the humble carrot should never be underestimated for its amazing nutritional benefits. Carrots are hearty vegetables that are easy to grow in all kinds of climates. They contain vitamins B, C, D, E, K and beta-carotene, and the minerals calcium, iron, phosphorus, chromium, magnesium, potassium and silica. Carrots are excellent for skin problems, and have been known to have great healing effects on ulcerous and inflamed conditions of the stomach and intestines.

VEGGIE-PACKED WINTER SLAW

WF DF GF SF VEG VG   SERVES 4

This delicious slaw topped with a flavoursome dressing is simple and speedy to prepare. A perfect salad to enjoy on warm summer evenings or plate it up at a picnic or potluck dinner. Any leftovers can be kept in the fridge, and will taste even better the next day.

1/4 small Savoy cabbage, thinly shredded

1/4 small purple cabbage, thinly shredded

1/2 bunch of kale, stems removed and leaves thinly shredded

2 carrots, shredded

25 g (1 oz/ 1/2 cup) chopped mint

2 tablespoons chia seeds

sprinkling of sesame seeds, to serve

DRESSING

65 g (21/4 oz/1/4 cup) tahini

6 drops stevia liquid, or 1 tablespoon rice malt syrup

1/2 teaspoon sesame oil

good pinch of Celtic sea salt, to taste

1 tablespoon apple cider vinegar

1 tablespoon freshly squeezed lemon juice

Place all the dressing ingredients in a small bowl with 60 ml (2 fl oz/1/4 cup) of filtered water and whisk with a fork.

Place the salad ingredients, except the sesame seeds, in a large bowl and coat with the dressing.

Scoop into awaiting bowls and serve sprinkled with the sesame seeds.

Health Benefits

Tahini is a rich source of vitamin A and methionine and contains lecithin, which reduces the levels of fat in the blood and is an environmental toxin protector. Tahini is a fantastic source of copper, magnesium, zinc, potassium, iron and phosphorus and an excellent source of calcium, too. Copper has been reported to be very good for rheumatoid arthritis sufferers, as it helps reduce pain and swelling.

EGGPLANT, POMEGRANATE AND MINTED QUINOA SALAD

WF DF GF VEG VG   SERVES 4–6

This salad will wow you with its beauty. Bright green mint contrasted with the bejewelling of gorgeous pink pomegranate seeds provides a lush experience for your eyes and your appetite. With its assortment of attractive colours comes a wide variety of antioxidants and micronutrients that will enhance your health naturally.

1 zucchini (courgette), sliced

1 eggplant (aubergine), cut into bite-sized pieces

4 garlic cloves, whole

80 ml (2^1/$_2$ fl oz/^{1}/$_3$ cup) cold-pressed extra virgin olive oil, plus extra, for drizzling

Celtic sea salt

270 g (9^1/$_2$ oz/1 cup) cooked quinoa

juice of 2 lemons

1 tablespoon grated lemon zest

1 bunch of mint, leaves only, plus extra, to serve

1 bunch of coriander (cilantro), leaves only, plus extra, to serve

1 pomegranate, seeds only

2 avocados, peeled, stones removed and sliced into wedges

4 small spring onions (scallions), chopped

125 g (4^1/$_2$ oz/1 cup) slivered almonds

Preheat the oven to 200°C (400°F/Gas 6).

Place the zucchini, eggplant and garlic on a baking tray, drizzle with olive oil, sprinkle with salt and roast for about 35 minutes.

Remove from the oven and set aside to cool.

Meanwhile, place the quinoa in a bowl with the lemon juice and zest and the olive oil. Combine well.

Place in a salad bowl with all the other ingredients and serve topped with extra mint and coriander leaves.

Health Benefits

Eggplant has vitamins and minerals in spades. It's rich in manganese, folic acid and all-important thiamine, the mineral that helps convert blood sugar into glucose for energy. Eggplant also contains a rare antioxidant known as nasunin. Found under the eggplant's skin, nasunin has been shown to protect brain cells from free-radical damage.

WARM BUCKWHEAT AND GOJI SALAD

● WF ● DF ● GF ● VEG ● VG   SERVES 2

Buckwheat is high in rutin, a flavonoid that protects against disease by strengthening capillaries and preventing blood clotting. It also contains high levels of magnesium, which relaxes blood vessels, improving blood flow and nutrient delivery and lowering blood pressure. It's the perfect ingredient for a healthy cardiovascular system.

160 g (5³/4 oz/1 cup) toasted buckwheat (kasha)

1 small onion, diced

1 small red capsicum (pepper), seeds and membrane removed, diced

1 small yellow capsicum (pepper), seeds and membrane removed, diced

1 tablespoon extra virgin coconut oil

100 g (3¹/2 oz/²/3 cup) pine nuts

2 carrots, shredded

2 handfuls of English spinach leaves

2 cups goji berries, to serve

DRESSING

1 tablespoon cold-pressed extra virgin olive oil

1¹/2 tablespoons freshly squeezed lemon juice

1 tablespoon chopped fresh or dried sage leaves

¹/2 teaspoon Celtic sea salt

freshly ground black pepper

Place the buckwheat in a saucepan along with 500 ml (17 fl oz/2 cups) of water. Bring to the boil then reduce the heat and simmer for 10–12 minutes, or follow the packet directions. Drain and set aside to cool in a large salad bowl.

Put the onion and capsicums in a frying pan with the coconut oil and fry until brown then add to the salad bowl.

Toast the pine nuts in a dry frying pan until golden, then set aside.

Whisk the dressing ingredients together.

Add the carrot and spinach to the salad bowl, pour over the dressing, season with salt and black pepper and scatter over the goji berries and pine nuts to serve.

MIXED LEAF SEEDED SALAD WITH CASHEW NUT MAYO

●WF ●DF ●GF ●SF ●VEG ●VG   SERVES 2

This magical mixed leaf and seeded salad will blow your preconceived ideas about 'boring salads' right out of the window. When choosing your mixed leaves, be sure to really go for variety, and plenty of deep green colours to get the maximum nutrient hit possible. Some of my favourite salad leaves are kale, spinach, rocket, beetroot leaves and cos lettuce. There are so many yummy varieties of greens out there; go nuts, because each different plant contains unique and powerful medicinal properties.

55 g (2 oz/^{1}/3 cup) sunflower seeds

55 g (2 oz/^{1}/3 cup) pepitas (pumpkin seeds)

50 g (1^3/4 oz/^{1}/3 cup) sesame seeds

2 cups mixed salad leaves

1 avocado, peeled, stone removed
   and cubed

2 tomatoes, julienned

1 cup snow peas (mangetout), sliced on
   the diagonal

freshly ground black pepper

CASHEW NUT MAYO

40 g (1^1/2 oz/^{1}/4 cup) raw cashews

2 teaspoons apple cider vinegar

pinch of Celtic sea salt

^{1}/4 shallot, finely diced

3 drops stevia liquid

Dry toast the seeds in a frying pan over medium heat for 3–5 minutes or until brown. Remove and set aside to cool.

Place the mayo ingredients in a food processor with 80 ml (2^1/2 fl oz/^{1}/3 cup) of filtered water and blend until smooth and creamy.

Arrange the salad ingredients in a bowl, reserving a few of the seeds to scatter on top.

Gently stir in the dressing to evenly coat the salad. Add the black pepper, the reserved seeds, and serve.

⤙ Health Benefits ⤚

Green leafies are probably one of the cheapest, most readily available superfoods on the planet. They're a fabulous plant-based source of non-haem iron, calcium, potassium, magnesium, vitamins A, C, K and E as well as several B vitamins. They're also high in fibre, and extremely rich in chlorophyll. Chlorophyll is a true all-rounder: it's incredibly alkalising; it enables the release of toxins from the body; it neutralises the pollution you breathe in; it oxygenates the body; and improves circulation by elevating your haemoglobin count.

TUSCAN KALESLAW

WF DF GF SF VEG VG   SERVES 3

All hail the mighty, illustrious kale; can it do no wrong? Whether you're already in a love affair with this powerful healing ingredient, or you're just in the courting stages, this crunchy kaleslaw will take your relationship to the next level.

3 cups thinly sliced Tuscan kale

1/2 cabbage, thinly sliced

1 red capsicum (pepper), seeds and
  membrane removed, thinly sliced

1 small carrot, grated

parsley, or micro herbs, to serve (optional)

DRESSING

120 g (41/4 oz/3/4 cup) raw cashews

40 g (11/2 oz/1/4 cup) sesame seeds

1 tablespoon freshly squeezed lemon juice

21/2 tablespoons apple cider vinegar

1/4 teaspoon Celtic sea salt

2 tablespoons sugar-free mustard

Place all the dressing ingredients in a food processor with a generous splash of filtered water and blend until smooth.

Place the slaw ingredients in a bowl, stir through the dressing and serve.

THE GARDENER'S BOUNTY

WF   DF   GF   SF   VEG   VG   SERVES 3

For the Rolls-Royce of nutrient-dense salads, look no further than The Gardener's Bounty. Overflowing with garden goodness, this salad is better than any multivitamin pill. This is your secret weapon against ill health, fatigue and lacklustre skin.

1 cup English spinach leaves

1 cup chopped kale, stem removed

1 cup rocket (arugula)

1 cup sugar snap peas

1 red capsicum (pepper), seeds and
   membrane removed, sliced

3 baby (pattypan) squash, quartered

1 small zucchini (courgette), thinly sliced

150 g (5¹/₂ oz/1 cup) cherry tomatoes

1 cucumber, cubed

DRESSING

60 ml (2 fl oz/¹/₄ cup) apple cider vinegar

1 garlic clove, sliced

1 teaspoon sugar-free mustard

¹/₂ teaspoon Celtic sea salt

125 ml (4 fl oz/¹/₂ cup) cold-pressed extra
   virgin olive oil

Assemble all the salad ingredients in a bowl.

Place all the dressing ingredients in a bowl and use a handheld blender to blend until smooth.

Pour the dressing over the salad and enjoy.

MUSHROOM WITH RED QUINOA SOUP

WF ● DF ● GF ● SF ● VEG ● VG   SERVES 4

This soup screams love and attention like a big protective hug. Warming and hearty, the mushrooms and quinoa muddle together, combining earthy and bold to bring your soup bowl alive with outstanding flavours.

1 tablespoon cold-pressed extra virgin olive oil

1 brown onion, finely diced

2 garlic cloves, finely chopped

2 large carrots, diced

1 tablespoon chopped rosemary leaves

1 teaspoon Celtic sea salt

freshly ground black pepper

750 g (1 lb 10 oz) button mushrooms, sliced

1.25 litres (44 fl oz/5 cups) vegetable stock

2 tablespoons wheat-free tamari

1 tablespoon apple cider vinegar

2 tablespoons tomato passata (puréed tomatoes)

50 g (1¾ oz/¼ cup) red quinoa

2 tablespoons nutritional yeast flakes, to serve

Heat the olive oil in a large saucepan over medium heat. Add the onion, garlic, carrot, rosemary and seasonings and sauté for 7 minutes, or until cooked through. Add the mushroom and cook for 5 minutes. Add the stock, tamari, apple cider vinegar, tomato passata and quinoa and cook for 20 minutes, or until the quinoa is soft.

Ladle into bowls and serve sprinkled with the nutritional yeast flakes.

LETTUCE AND COCONUT SOUP

WF DF GF SF VEG VG   SERVES 4

Lettuce needn't be limited to salads. Gently heated and blended, it creates a lovely texture in a soup, as well as adding some extra vitamins and minerals. Iceberg lettuce is perfect, as it doesn't have the bitterness of some other greens, and is also high in water. This soup is simple and light; a perfect starter or afternoon pick-me-up.

1 tablespoon extra virgin coconut oil

2 garlic cloves, crushed

1 brown onion, chopped

1 litre (35 fl oz/4 cups) vegetable stock

1 iceberg lettuce, roughly chopped

1 teaspoon Celtic sea salt

freshly ground black pepper

60 ml (2 fl oz/¼ cup) additive-free coconut milk, plus extra, to serve

parsley, to serve (optional)

Heat the coconut oil in a large heavy-based saucepan over medium heat and add the garlic and onion. Cook for 3–5 minutes, then add the stock. Bring to the boil then reduce the heat to low and simmer for about 5 minutes. Add the lettuce and simmer for 10 minutes. Season with salt and pepper.

Remove from the heat and purée with a handheld blender. Return to the heat, add the coconut milk and cook, stirring, until heated through.

Transfer to bowls, swirl through the extra coconut milk and top with parsley, if using, to serve.

CELERY, CASHEW AND LEEK SOUP

WF · DF · GF · SF · VEG · VG   SERVES 4

I'm constantly surprised by the versatility of cashews. Whether added to sweet or savoury dishes, their crunch and creaminess bring a sense of satisfaction. Blended into this amazing soup, the impressive cashew provides a distinct, buttery smoothness.

1 tablespoon cold-pressed extra virgin olive oil

4 garlic cloves, sliced

1 leek, white part only, trimmed, washed and chopped

1½ heads celery, sliced into 5 mm (¼ inch) chunks

2 cardamom pods

1 litre (35 fl oz/4 cups) vegetable stock

155 g (5½ oz/1 cup) cashews (reserve 50 g (1¾ oz/⅓ cup) for garnish)

125 ml (4 fl oz/½ cup) additive-free coconut milk

Heat the olive oil in a large heavy-based saucepan over medium heat and sauté the garlic and leek for 3–5 minutes. Add the celery and cardamom pods and cook for a further 5 minutes. Add the stock, bring to the boil and then lower the heat and simmer for 15 minutes or until the celery is tender.

Remove from the heat and place in a blender with the cashews. Blend until smooth.

Return to the saucepan over low heat and add the coconut milk, cooking until it is warmed through.

Serve topped with the reserved cashews.

MOROCCAN PUMPKIN SOUP

WF • DF • GF • SF • VEG • VG   SERVES 3

Immerse yourself in the magic of Morocco with this delightful bowl of delectability. A melting pot of nurturing spices, this exotic vegetarian feast will quell your hunger and ignite your senses.

2 tablespoons cold-pressed extra virgin olive oil

1 brown onion, chopped

2 garlic cloves, finely chopped

500 g (1 lb 2 oz) butternut pumpkin (squash), diced

400 g (14 oz) tin chickpeas

1 litre (35 fl oz/4 cups) vegetable stock

7 drops stevia liquid

juice and zest of 1 lemon

1/2 teaspoon ground cinnamon

1/4 teaspoon ginger

1/4 teaspoon turmeric

1/4 teaspoon nutmeg

Celtic sea salt and freshly ground black pepper

1/4 cup coriander (cilantro) leaves, chopped

Add the olive oil to a large saucepan over medium–low heat and sauté the onion and garlic for 3–5 minutes, until soft and translucent. Add the pumpkin, chickpeas, stock, stevia, lemon juice and zest, spices and salt and pepper and simmer, partially covered, for 20 minutes, or until the pumpkin is tender.

To serve, ladle into bowls and top with the chopped coriander.

⅌ Supercharged Tip ⅌

This soup can be blended in a food processor for a smoother result.

ZESTY VEGAN THAI SOUP

WF DF GF SF VEG VG   SERVES 4

A Thai chef's pantry is like a medicinal treasure chest. This aromatic, vegan-friendly soup is the perfect meal in my eyes: big on flavour and full of healing ingredients like galangal, kaffir lime leaves and coriander.

750 ml (26 fl oz/3 cups) vegetable stock

7.5 cm (3 inch) piece of galangal, grated

2 lemongrass stems, peeled and white part only, cut into 2 cm (3/4 inch) pieces

3–4 kaffir lime leaves, torn

4 spring onions (scallions), shredded lengthways

7 drops stevia liquid

400 ml (14 fl oz) additive-free coconut milk

3–4 red chillies, finely chopped

1 tablespoon apple cider vinegar

2 tablespoons wheat-free tamari

2 carrots, shredded

1 red capsicum (pepper), seeds and membrane removed, sliced

90 g (3 1/4 oz/1 cup) thinly sliced button mushrooms

60 ml (2 fl oz/1/4 cup) lime juice

zest of 1 lime

4 tablespoons coriander (cilantro) leaves, to serve (optional)

Add the vegetable stock to a stockpot over high heat. Bring to the boil then add the galangal, lemongrass, lime leaves, spring onion and stevia. Reduce the heat to medium and simmer for 5 minutes. Add the coconut milk, chillies, apple cider vinegar, tamari and carrot and simmer for 10 minutes. Add the capsicum and mushroom and cook for a further 5 minutes.

Remove the soup from the heat and add the lime juice and zest.

Ladle into bowls and garnish with the coriander, if using.

GREEN BEAUTY SOUP

WF   DF   GF   SF   VEG   VG   SERVES 3

Greens with benefits. A top-notch super bowl of seasonal ingredients with a punchy taste and fabulous colour. This dish has the flexibility for you to use your favourite fresh ingredients.

1 tablespoon cold-pressed extra virgin olive oil

1 onion, chopped

1 leek, white part only, trimmed, washed and chopped

3 garlic cloves, chopped

2 celery stalks, sliced

2 heads of broccoli, chopped

1 bunch of kale, stems removed and leaves chopped

500 ml (17 fl oz/2 cups) vegetable stock

400 ml (14 fl oz) additive-free coconut milk

pinch of Celtic sea salt

freshly ground black pepper, to taste

2 tablespoons freshly squeezed lemon juice, to serve

nutritional yeast flakes, to serve

Heat the olive oil in a large heavy-based saucepan over medium heat and brown the onion, leek, garlic and celery for 7 minutes. Add the broccoli and kale and stir-fry for 5 minutes. Pour in the stock and coconut milk and bring to the boil. Reduce the heat and simmer for 15–20 minutes. Remove from the heat and allow to cool slightly.

Transfer to a blender and blend until smooth.

Return the soup to the saucepan and gently reheat. Season to taste.

To serve, stir in the lemon juice and sprinkle with nutritional yeast flakes.

SPRING LENTIL AND VEGETABLE SOUP

WF   DF   GF   SF   VEG   VG   SERVES 3

If you want to be wise with your wallet, lentils are your ultimate pantry staple. This dish is incredibly simple to put together, and proves that you needn't break the bank in the name of good health.

2 tablespoons cold-pressed extra virgin olive oil

1 brown onion, chopped

2 large carrots, chopped

1 celeriac, chopped

1 medium turnip, peeled and chopped

475 g (1 lb 1 oz/2¼ cups) lentils, soaked in water for 45 minutes

1 tablespoon fresh mixed herbs, such as parsley, sage, rosemary, thyme

1.5 litres (52 fl oz/6 cups) vegetable stock

1 large bunch of kale, stems removed, leaves coarsely chopped

Celtic sea salt and freshly ground black pepper

Heat the olive oil in a large heavy-based saucepan over high heat and sauté the onion, carrot, celeriac and turnip for 10 minutes.

Stir in the lentils, herbs, stock and kale and bring to the boil, stirring. Reduce the heat to medium–low, cover loosely with a lid and simmer for about 20 minutes, or until the lentils are tender, stirring occasionally.

Season with salt and pepper, then serve.

CREAMY SUMMER HERB SOUP

WF   DF   GF   SF   VEG   VG   SERVES 4

A seasonal soup is the perfect way to use up leftover veggies. In the balmy summer months, this light combination will showcase the beautiful abundance of garden-fresh goodness that is on offer, while supplying you with a mix of easily digested nutrients to keep your insides happy.

2 tablespoons extra virgin coconut oil

1 brown onion, chopped

3 garlic cloves, crushed

1/2 cauliflower, chopped into florets

1 litre (35 fl oz/4 cups) vegetable stock

400 ml (14 fl oz) additive-free coconut milk

2 cups fresh mixed herbs, such as basil, parsley, sage, chives, dill, tarragon, finely chopped

4 thyme sprigs

1/4 cup watercress, roughly chopped

1 cup chopped English spinach leaves

1 tablespoon freshly squeezed lemon juice

Celtic sea salt and freshly ground black pepper

pinch of nutmeg

thyme sprigs, to serve

Heat the coconut oil in a large heavy-based saucepan and sauté the onion and garlic for 3–5 minutes, until soft. Add the cauliflower and sauté for 7 minutes, or until brown. Add the stock and coconut milk and simmer for a few minutes. Add the herbs, watercress, spinach and lemon juice, reduce the heat to very low, partially cover and simmer for 10 minutes. Take care that the soup does not boil.

Season with salt and pepper and add the nutmeg. Serve immediately, garnished with a sprig of thyme.

⚶Supercharged Tip⚶

If you prefer a smoother soup, you can blend this to your desired consistency.

ZUCCHINI NOODLE (ZOODLE) SOUP

WF ● DF ● GF ● SF ● VEG ● VG   SERVES 4

There are oodles of zoodles in this slurpable soup, just like Grandma used to make. The trick is to use the best quality ingredients your farmers' market can supply, and if you have homemade stock on hand, that's even better.

1¹/₂ tablespoons extra virgin coconut oil

1 brown onion, chopped

2 celery stalks, chopped

2 carrots, thinly sliced

3 garlic cloves, minced

1.5 litres (52 fl oz/6 cups) vegetable stock

1 tablespoon thyme leaves

Celtic sea salt and freshly ground black pepper, to taste

2 large zucchini (courgettes), spiralised into noodles or cut into thin ribbons

Heat the coconut oil in a large heavy-based saucepan over medium heat and cook the onion, celery, carrot and garlic for 5–7 minutes, or until the onion is translucent. Add the stock, thyme and salt and pepper and bring to the boil. Reduce the heat and simmer for 30 minutes.

To make the zoodles, wash the zucchini and spiralise, using a vegetable spiraliser or spirooli machine. If you don't have a spiraliser, use a vegetable peeler to make ribbon-strip zoodles.

Add the zoodles to the pan, remove from the heat and let it stand for a few minutes before serving – the heat of the soup will cook the zoodles through.

CURRIED PARSNIP SOUP

WF   DF   GF   SF   VEG   VG   SERVES 3

This is a subtle, aromatic bowl of earthy soup, with a sweet, exotic and nutty flavour, perfect for any season. This soup makes a fragrant log-cabin fireside supper.

1 tablespoon cold-pressed extra virgin olive oil

1 brown onion, finely chopped

2 garlic cloves, finely chopped

4–5 parsnips, cubed

1 teaspoon curry powder

2 teaspoons turmeric

1 teaspoon grated lemon zest

1 litre (35 fl oz/4 cups) vegetable stock

125 ml (4 fl oz/1/2 cup) additive-free coconut milk

Celtic sea salt and freshly ground black pepper

handful of coriander (cilantro) leaves, to garnish

Heat the olive oil in a large saucepan over medium–high heat. Add the onion and garlic and cook for 3–5 minutes. Add the parsnip and sauté for 5–7 minutes, then add the curry powder, turmeric and lemon zest. Lower the heat and simmer, covered, for 10–15 minutes, stirring regularly. Add the stock and bring to the boil. Reduce the heat and simmer for about 25 minutes, or until the parsnip is cooked through.

Transfer the soup to a bowl and, using a handheld blender, purée until smooth. Return to the pan, add the coconut milk, season with salt and pepper and cook, stirring, until heated through.

Serve garnished with coriander and with Happy Kale Chips (see page 190) on the side.

BUCKWHEAT MINESTRONE

● WF ● DF ● GF ● SF ● VEG ● VG   SERVES 4

Minestrone literally means 'big soup', and this bowl of seasonal shape-shifters does not disappoint. A handy and versatile buckwheat-based soup combining myriad life-enhancing vegetables and gluten-free spirals which offers a rollercoaster ride of joy and pleasure.

2 tablespoons extra virgin coconut oil

1 large onion, diced

3 garlic cloves, sliced

1 small red capsicum (pepper), seeds and
   membrane removed, diced

1 large carrot, diced

1 celery stalk, diced

400 g (14 oz) tin diced tomatoes

1/2 cauliflower, chopped into florets

2 zucchini (courgettes), diced

1 teaspoon tomato passata (puréed tomato)

1 tablespoon apple cider vinegar

1 tablespoon lime juice

1 teaspoon dried oregano

2 litres (70 fl oz/8 cups) vegetable stock

120 g (4 1/4 oz) buckwheat pasta spirals

Celtic sea salt and freshly ground
   black pepper

2 tablespoons nutritional yeast flakes

Heat the coconut oil in a large heavy-based saucepan over medium heat and sauté the onion, garlic, capsicum, carrot and celery for about 10 minutes, or until the vegetables have softened. Add the tomatoes, cauliflower, zucchini, tomato passata, apple cider vinegar, lime juice, oregano and stock and bring to the boil. Reduce the heat and simmer, covered, for 15–20 minutes. Add the buckwheat spirals, season with salt and pepper, and cook for a further 10 minutes, stirring occasionally.

Serve topped with the nutritional yeast flakes.

PEA SOUP FOR THE SOUL

WF ◦ DF ◦ GF ◦ SF ◦ VEG ◦ VG   SERVES 3–4

The sweetness of this soup comes from pre-roasting the garlic bulb in the oven. Simmering the soup on the stove increases the flavour ten-fold; if you're not pushed for time, let it simmer for 15 minutes before blending.

1 garlic bulb (corm)

60 ml (2 fl oz/1/4 cup) cold-pressed extra virgin olive oil, plus extra, to serve

1 brown onion, diced

3 thyme sprigs, leaves only

1 litre (35 fl oz/4 cups) vegetable stock

500 g (1 lb 2 oz) fresh or frozen peas

1 tablespoon apple cider vinegar

Celtic sea salt and freshly ground black pepper

handful of parsley leaves, plus extra, to serve

Preheat the oven to 200°C (400°F/Gas 6).

Cut the top off the garlic bulb, place on a baking tray, drizzle with 1 tablespoon of the olive oil and bake for 30–35 minutes.

Meanwhile, heat the remaining 2 tablespoons of olive oil in a large saucepan over medium heat and cook the onion and thyme for 5 minutes. Add the stock, peas, apple cider vinegar, salt and pepper and bring to the boil. Reduce the heat to low, add the parsley and simmer gently, partially covered, for 5–10 minutes. (Cook for longer if you would like a stronger flavour.)

Remove from the heat and place in a blender.

Remove the garlic from the oven and squeeze the garlic cloves out of their skins. Add to the blender and blend until smooth.

Serve sprinkled with the extra parsley leaves and a drizzle of extra virgin olive oil.

Health Benefits

Peas really are the bees' knees. Their juice is highly beneficial for people with gluten intolerance, as it repairs the membranes in the small intestine that can prevent fats being absorbed. Peas are also rich in protein, fibre, iron and vitamins A, C and B1 (thiamine), which is essential for energy production, nerve function and carbohydrate metabolism. The water-soluble fibres in peas bind with cholesterol and help excrete the baddies from the body, promoting intestinal health.

TOMATO AND BEETROOT SOUP

WF DF GF SF VEG VG   SERVES 2

A divine, warming and flavourful soup that's impossible to get wrong. Add some good-looking mint leaves for garnish. It's also delicious served with the Pesto on page 194.

2 tablespoons cold-pressed extra virgin olive oil

1 garlic clove, finely chopped

1 large beetroot, peeled and cut into 2.5 cm (1 inch) cubes

4–5 tomatoes, cut into quarters

1 tablespoon apple cider vinegar

1/4 teaspoon stevia liquid, or 1 tablespoon rice malt syrup

1/4 teaspoon Celtic sea salt

freshly ground black pepper

mint leaves, to garnish

Heat the olive oil in a large heavy-based saucepan over medium heat. Add the garlic and beetroot and cook for 1 minute. Add the tomatoes and cook, stirring, for a further 5 minutes. Add the apple cider vinegar, stevia liquid or rice malt syrup and season with salt and pepper to taste.

Remove from the heat and transfer to a food processor. Blend until smooth.

Serve garnished with mint leaves.

MAIN MEALS, BOWLS AND BOARDS

Create your own game-changing super bowls, perfectly proportioned sharing meals for your chopping board, and plant-based plates for every night of the week. Whether you're entertaining a crowd or making dinner for one, here you'll find a selection of delectable dishes that will become firm favourites, such as stir-fries, crusty pizza, moussaka and pastas. This is a chapter where every dish is overflowing with goodness, love and the joys of eating simply.

QUINOA SAN CHOY BOW

WF   DF   GF   SF   VEG   VG   SERVES 4

My favourite thing about this bright and zingy vegetarian san choy bow is that it packs loads of flavour and has a wonderfully authentic taste. The other good news is that you won't be hungry five minutes later, have to deal with dodgy, chemically-laden additives or be met with idiomatic fortune cookies if you make it yourself.

2 tablespoons sesame oil

115 g (4 oz/1 cup) bean sprouts

60 g (2¼ oz oz/½ cup) chopped green beans

1 carrot, diced

1 red capsicum (pepper), seeds and membrane removed, chopped

1 green capsicum (pepper), seeds and membrane removed, chopped

1 celery stalk, diced

2 red chillies, finely chopped

3 garlic cloves, diced

1 large piece of ginger, finely grated

270 g (9½ oz/1 cup) cooked quinoa

1 tablespoon apple cider vinegar

3 tablespoons wheat-free tamari

1 tablespoon freshly squeezed lemon juice

Celtic sea salt and freshly ground black pepper

8 chilled iceberg lettuce leaves

2 teaspoons chopped coriander (cilantro) leaves

1 tablespoon toasted sesame seeds

3–4 spring onions (scallions), chopped

Heat the sesame oil in a wok or frying pan over medium heat and add the bean sprouts, green beans, carrot, capsicum, celery, chilli, garlic and ginger. Stir-fry for 7–10 minutes or until slightly browned. Add the quinoa, apple cider vinegar, tamari and lemon juice and cook for 2 minutes. Season with salt and pepper to taste.

Remove from the heat and spoon the mixture into the lettuce. Garnish with the coriander leaves, toasted sesame seeds and spring onions and enjoy.

Health Benefits

Quinoa has many nutritional benefits: it's high in protein, low in carbohydrates, gluten-free, has a low GI and is an easy ingredient to digest. When cooking quinoa, remember to rinse it well and cook for approximately 12 minutes until all the water has been absorbed. You can also cook quinoa in stock or with herbs to create a flavoursome base for any meal.

SUPERCHARGED PAD THAI

◆WF ◗DF ♥GF ◖SF ◆VEG ◗VG   SERVES 4

If you find yourself craving Thai, whip up this quick and easy raw Pad Thai. Overflowing with freshness and brimming with the immune-boosting, detoxifying properties of ginger, coriander and garlic, this zucchini-noodle version is the height of deliciousness.

1 red capsicum (pepper), seeds and membrane removed, cut into thin strips

2 spring onions (scallions), chopped

4–5 zucchini (courgettes), spiralised into noodles or cut into thin ribbons

1 large carrot

1/4 cabbage, shredded

230 g (81/2 oz/2 cups) bean sprouts, to serve

10 g (1/4 oz/1/3 cup) coriander (cilantro) leaves, to serve

120 g (41/4 oz/3/4 cup) activated nuts, such as cashews and almonds, crushed, to serve

lime wedges, to serve

DRESSING

60 ml (2 fl oz/1/4 cup) additive-free coconut milk

1 tablespoon olive oil

60 ml (2 fl oz/1/4 cup) wheat-free soy sauce

21/2 tablespoons tahini

2 tablespoons freshly squeezed lemon juice

2 garlic cloves, minced

1 red chilli, finely chopped

1 teaspoon grated ginger

6 drops stevia liquid

Place the capsicum, spring onion, zucchini, carrot and cabbage in a large bowl and combine.

Combine the dressing ingredients in a jar and shake well.

Pour the dressing over the vegetables, mixing to ensure they are evenly coated.

Serve with the bean sprouts, coriander, activated nuts and lime wedges.

LETTUCE LEAF TACOS

●WF ●DF ●GF ●SF ●VEG ●VG   SERVES 4

Gather the amigos for these vibrant lettuce leaf tacos that skip the cheap and nasty ingredients.

SALSA

2 teaspoons cold-pressed extra virgin olive oil

1 onion, finely chopped

2 garlic cloves, crushed

1/2 teaspoon Celtic sea salt

1 bunch of basil, chopped

small handful of mint, chopped

7 tomatoes, diced

juice of 1 lime

1 yellow capsicum (pepper), seeds and
    membrane removed, finely diced

1 red chilli, finely chopped

TACO FILLING

230 g (81/2 oz/2 cups) walnuts

2 tablespoons wheat-free tamari

1 teaspoon ground cumin

1 teaspoon extra virgin olive oil

SUNFLOWER SEED CHEESE

145 g (5 oz/1 cup) sunflower seeds, soaked
    in water overnight

2 garlic cloves

juice of 1/2 lemon

1/2 teaspoon Celtic sea salt

TO SERVE

4 cos (romaine) lettuce leaves, washed
    and dried

1 avocado, peeled, stone removed and
    cubed (optional)

1 tablespoon nutritional yeast flakes

lime wedges (optional)

To make the salsa, heat the olive oil in a small frying pan over medium heat and fry the onion for about 6 minutes, or until lightly brown. Add the garlic and fry for a further 2–3 minutes, or until it starts to change colour. Transfer to a bowl and set aside to cool.

Once the onion mixture has cooled, add the salt, basil, mint, tomatoes, lime juice, capsicum and chilli. Set aside for an hour or so to allow the flavours to infuse.

To make the filling, soak the walnuts in filtered water for 2 hours.

Place all the filling ingredients in a food processor and blend until it reaches a crumbly consistency. Don't blend for too long or it will turn into nut butter.

To make the sunflower seed cheese, place the seeds, garlic, lemon juice and salt in a food processor and blend until a smooth paste forms. Add a little filtered water to reach the desired consistency. Set aside in the fridge for a minimum of 30 minutes before serving.

To serve, spread the lettuce leaves on a serving platter. Add the filling, salsa, avocado, if using, and sunflower seed cheese. Sprinkle with the nutritional yeast flakes, season with salt and black pepper, and serve with lime wedges, if desired, on the side.

MUCHOS NACHOS

WF DF GF SF VEG   SERVES 3–4

Nachos are the ultimate chopping-board meal. Scatter chips in a basket, then decorate your board with small bowls of diced tomatoes and cucumber, Cashew Sour Cream and Creamy Avocado Dressing, ready for a free-for-all.

To veganise: Substitute the egg with 3 tablespoons ground or whole chia or flaxseeds soaked in 125 ml (4 fl oz/1/2 cup) of water for 15 minutes.

2 tomatoes, diced

1 cucumber, diced

Cashew Sour Cream, see page 217

Creamy Avocado Dressing, see page 218

coriander (cilantro) sprigs, to serve

NACHOS CHIPS

100 g (3 1/2 oz/1 cup) almond meal

1 large organic egg

1 teaspoon turmeric

1/4 teaspoon cumin

1/4 teaspoon coriander

1 teaspoon grated orange zest

1 teaspoon Celtic sea salt

To make the chips, preheat the oven to 180°C (350°F/Gas 4).

Place all the chip ingredients in a large bowl and mix with a wooden spoon to form a dough.

Place the dough on a clean work surface between two pieces of baking paper. Roll the dough out until it is 2 mm (1/16 inch) thick.

Remove the top piece of baking paper and transfer the dough and bottom piece of baking paper to a baking tray. Using a sharp knife, deeply score the dough every 3 cm (1 1/4 inch), then do the same in the opposite direction so you form squares.

Bake in the oven for 12 minutes.

Allow to cool before breaking them apart.

To assemble the nachos, place the Nachos chips on a chopping board, and top with the remaining ingredients.

Any leftover chips will keep in an airtight container for up to 3 days.

NUTRITIOUS ASIAN BOWL

WF DF GF SF VEG VG   SERVES 2

Personalising this dish allows you to bring your local Asian restaurant home to your kitchen, and combines spectacular Japanese flavours with highly nutritious vegetarian ingredients.

430 g (15¼ oz/2⅓ cups) cooked brown rice

DRESSING

2 tablespoons apple cider vinegar

1 tablespoon wheat-free tamari

1 tablespoon sesame oil

60 ml (2 fl oz/¼ cup) freshly squeezed lemon juice

TOPPINGS

1 tablespoon cold-pressed extra virgin olive oil

1 cup mushrooms

1 cucumber, cubed

1 avocado, peeled, stone removed and sliced

½ cup steamed edamame

1 carrot, shredded

1 small red capsicum (pepper), seeds and membrane removed, diced

½ cup finely chopped daikon

1 teaspoon grated ginger

1 serving of Happy Kale Chips, see page 190

2 tablespoons toasted sesame seeds

To make the dressing, whisk the dressing ingredients together in a small bowl. Set aside.

Pan-fry the mushrooms in olive oil for 5 minutes.

Divide the rice between two bowls. Pour over the dressing, add all the topping ingredients and serve.

BROWN LENTIL CHILLI BOWL

WF DF GF SF VEG VG   SERVES 3–4

If you find yourself feeling a little lacklustre at times, then why not add some spice to your meals? This dish is sure to boost your circulation, and will warm you up when the temperature goes down.

1 tablespoon cold-pressed extra virgin olive oil

1 brown onion, chopped

4 garlic cloves, finely chopped

1 red capsicum (pepper), seeds and membrane removed, chopped

1 tablespoon chilli powder

1 tablespoon ground cumin

430 g (15¼ oz/2 cups) brown lentils, soaked in water overnight then drained

400 g (14 oz) tin diced tomatoes

1.5 litres (52 fl oz/6 cups) vegetable stock

¼ cup coriander (cilantro) leaves

yoghurt, to serve (optional)

2 tablespoons nutritional yeast flakes

Heat the olive oil in a large saucepan over medium–high heat. Add the onion, garlic and capsicum and sauté for 5 minutes. Add the chilli powder and and cumin and stir to combine. Add the lentils, tomatoes and stock and bring to the boil. Reduce the heat to medium–low and simmer, partially covered, for 30 minutes or until the lentils are almost tender. Remove the lid and cook for a further 10 minutes.

To serve, stir through the coriander and top with a dollop of yoghurt, if using, and the nutritional yeast flakes.

CREAMY CURRIED CAULIFLOWER WITH CASHEWS

●WF ●DF ●GF ●SF ●VEG ●VG　　SERVES 3

Wave goodbye to soggy cauliflower, and say hello to a spicy and delicious aromatic curry. Flavoursome florets soak up the masala beautifully and transport you to Bollywood with every mouthful.

2 tablespoons extra virgin coconut oil

1 onion, chopped

2 garlic cloves, minced

1 tablespoon finely chopped ginger

1 tablespoon curry powder

2 teaspoons turmeric

1 teaspoon ground cinnamon

2 teaspoons cumin

1 large cauliflower, cut into florets

570 ml (20 fl oz) additive-free coconut milk

2 teaspoons grated lemon zest

155 g (5 1/2 oz/1 cup) raw cashews

Celtic sea salt and freshly ground black pepper, to taste

3 tablespoons chopped coriander (cilantro) leaves

555 g (1 lb 4 oz/3 cups) cooked brown rice, to serve

Melt the coconut oil in a large saucepan over medium heat. Add the onion and cook for 3–5 minutes. Add the garlic, ginger, curry powder, turmeric, cinnamon and cumin and stir for 1 minute, until the spices are fragrant. Add the cauliflower, coconut milk, lemon zest, cashews and salt and bring to the boil. Reduce the heat and simmer, covered, for 15–20 minutes.

Finish with salt and pepper, coriander leaves and serve with brown rice.

⚜ Health Benefits ⚜

Cauliflower is nutrient-rich and loaded with vitamin K, folate, fibre and antioxidants. Its benefits are manifold, and include maintaining excellent blood flow for the heart and kidneys, reducing inflammation and strengthening the immune system.

BUCKWHEAT STUFFED CAPSICUMS

● WF ● DF ● GF ● SF ● VEG ● VG   MAKES 2

If you're looking to feast on food that nurtures and heals your body, bringing you increased vitality, energy and more get-up-and-go, then look no further than this dish. It's a lovely on-demand miracle meal which is full-flavoured and foolproof, bursting with appealing nutrient-rich ingredients to boost your immune system and keep you in tip-top shape. Spice up your life and stuff it with flavour and colour. If you don't have buckwheat, fear not! Brown rice will suffice.

1 red capsicum (pepper), seeds and
  membrane removed

1 yellow capsicum (pepper), seeds and
  membrane removed

135 g (4³/4 oz/²/3 cup) buckwheat, rinsed

1 tablespoon extra virgin coconut oil

1 onion, finely chopped

1 garlic clove, crushed

1 teaspoon cumin seeds

1/4 teaspoon cayenne pepper

1/2 red chilli, seeded and finely
  chopped (optional)

1 teaspoon ground coriander

1 teaspoon freshly grated ginger

400 g (14 oz) tin diced tomatoes

2 teaspoons apple cider vinegar

pinch of Celtic sea salt

freshly ground black pepper

1 tablespoon cold-pressed extra
  virgin olive oil

basil leaves, to garnish

Preheat the oven to 220°C (425°F/Gas 7).

Bring a large saucepan of filtered water to the boil, reduce the heat to a simmer and cook the capsicums for 3–4 minutes. Carefully remove the capsicums with a slotted spoon and drain well.

Meanwhile, bring the buckwheat to the boil in a saucepan of water. Reduce the heat and simmer for about 12 minutes, or until tender – take care to not overcook it.

Heat the coconut oil in a large frying pan over medium heat and sauté the onion and garlic for 3–6 minutes. Move to one side of the pan and add the cumin seeds to the other side, toasting them until they pop. Stir to combine them with the onion and garlic. Add the cayenne pepper, chilli, if using, coriander, ginger, tomatoes, apple cider vinegar and salt and pepper and cook for 10 minutes. Remove from the heat.

Drain the buckwheat and add to the tomato mixture, stirring gently to combine.

Add the stuffing mixture to the capsicums, taking care not to overstuff them.

Brush the capsicums with the olive oil and cook in the oven for 20–25 minutes.

Sprinkle with basil and serve.

⊱ Health Benefits ⊰

Buckwheat is high in naturally occurring B-complex vitamins that provide your body with energy.

COCONUT MUSHROOMS WITH CAULIFLOWER RICE

●WF ◐DF ●GF ●SF ◐VEG ●VG   SERVES 2

Mushrooms are a must-have in any plant-lover's pantry. This recipe pairs their deliciously earthy flavour with the sweetness of coconut. A mouthwatering combination.

2 tablespoons extra virgin coconut oil

4 cups mushrooms, sliced

2.5 cm (1 inch) piece of ginger, grated

2 garlic cloves, chopped

2 tablespoons wheat-free tamari

3 tablespoons unsweetened coconut flakes

juice of 1/2 lime

1 tablespoon lime zest

green salad, to serve

CAULIFLOWER RICE

1 small cauliflower, cut into florets

pinch of Celtic sea salt

freshly ground black pepper

2 tablespoons cold-pressed extra virgin olive oil

2 garlic cloves, minced

To make the cauliflower rice, place the cauliflower in a food processor and pulse to a fine grain. Season with salt and pepper.

Heat the olive oil in a frying pan over medium–high heat and cooked the cauliflower for 5–7 minutes, or until *al dente*.

Meanwhile, melt the coconut oil in a large frying pan over high heat and cook the mushrooms for 5 minutes. Add the ginger and garlic and sauté for 3–5 minutes. Add the tamari and stir to combine. Add the coconut flakes, lime juice and zest and reduce the heat to medium then cook for 10 minutes.

Transfer the mushrooms to a bowl and serve on a chopping board, accompanied by the cauliflower rice and a crispy green salad.

CELERIAC PASTA WITH HERBED TOMATO SAUCE

WF ⬥ DF ⬥ GF ⬥ SF ⬥ VEG ⬥ VG   SERVES 4

If you need a change from zucchini linguini, then why not introduce a new vegetable pasta into your repertoire? You should never judge a book by its cover and, although it's not the prettiest vegetable in the bunch and a bit nobbly, celeriac makes a beautiful ribbon pasta when thinly sliced. It has a wonderfully creamy and slightly nutty taste, and partners perfectly with herbed tomato sauce or puttanesca.

1 celeriac, peeled

500 ml (17 fl oz/2 cups) vegetable stock

HERBED TOMATO SAUCE

2 tablespoons cold-pressed extra virgin olive oil

1 red capsicum (pepper), seeds and membrane removed, very finely chopped

2 garlic cloves, crushed

1 onion, chopped

7 whole tomatoes, peeled and chopped (see note)

3 tablespoons tomato paste (concentrated purée)

6 drops stevia liquid

1/2 teaspoon Celtic sea salt

freshly ground black pepper

1 tablespoon chopped mixed basil and parsley

To make the tomato sauce, heat the olive oil in a large heavy-based frying pan over medium heat. Add the capsicum, garlic and onion and cook, stirring often, for 6–8 minutes or until the onion is translucent. Add the tomatoes, tomato paste, stevia, salt and a few grinds of black pepper. Bring to the boil, cover and simmer for 20 minutes or until the sauce thickens. Stir in the basil and parsley and taste for salt and pepper, adjusting if necessary. Set aside to cool.

Meanwhile, to make the pasta, use a mandolin or knife to cut the celeriac into fine ribbons. Heat the vegetable stock to a simmer. Place the celeriac in the simmering stock and cook for 3 minutes, or until tender.

Serve the pasta topped with the tomato sauce.

NOTE: The tomato sauce will keep in the fridge in a sterile, tightly sealed jar for up to a week. It can also be frozen for up to a month in a sealed container. To peel the tomatoes, carefully make a slit down one side of each tomato and place in a large bowl. Top with boiling water, ensuring they are well covered, then leave them for a few minutes. Before straining off the water, test one to ensure that they are ready – the skin should peel off easily. If it does, strain the tomatoes and allow to cool before peeling them.

Health Benefits

Celeriac is bursting with calcium and magnesium and immune system–enhancing zinc. It contains water-soluble fibre which helps to lower cholesterol, and is also beneficial to the nervous, lymphatic and urinary systems.

WINTER VEGETABLE KORMA

WF   DF   GF   SF   VEG   VG   SERVES 5

When the crisp winter air begins to creep into your life, you will find consolation in this hearty korma. It's the perfect comfort food, packed with seasonal veg and a range of immune-boosting spices to ward off winter bugs.

40 g (1½ oz/¼ cup) raw, unsalted cashews

40 g (1½ oz/¼ cup) blanched almonds

400 ml (14 fl oz) additive-free coconut milk

¼ teaspoon ground cinnamon

¾ teaspoon ground fennel seeds

1 teaspoon red chilli flakes

1 tablespoon ground turmeric

1 tablespoon ground coriander

1 teaspoon ground cardamom

3 teaspoons curry powder

1½ tablespoons extra virgin coconut oil

1 brown onion, chopped

6 garlic cloves, crushed

2.5 cm (1 inch) piece of ginger, grated

1 large tomato, diced

1 cauliflower, florets chopped

1 large turnip, diced

2 carrots, diced

90 g (3¼ oz/¾ cup) green beans, sliced

80 g (2¾ oz/½ cup) green peas

pinch of Celtic sea salt

freshly ground black pepper, to taste

¼ cup coriander (cilantro) leaves, to serve

15 g (½ oz/¼ cup) toasted unsweetened coconut flakes, to serve

Place the cashews and almonds in a bowl, cover with filtered water and soak for 2 hours.

Place the nuts in a food processor with the coconut milk and blend.

Combine the spices in a small bowl and mix well.

Heat the coconut oil in a large heavy-based saucepan over high heat and sauté the onion, garlic and ginger for 4–5 minutes. Add the mixed spices to the pan and cook, stirring, for 1 minute or until the spices are aromatic. Add the tomato and cook for a further minute, stirring. Add the remaining vegetables to the pan with the coconut milk sauce and cook for 10 minutes. Season to taste with salt and pepper.

Reduce the heat to medium and cook for a further 35–45 minutes, adding filtered water if necessary.

Remove from the heat and serve topped with coriander and coconut flakes.

PUMPKIN CURRY WITH BROWN RICE

WF · DF · GF · SF · VEG · VG   SERVES 2

You don't have to be daunted by curries — this recipe is simple to make and delivers a winning result without the fuss. In India, it is not uncommon to eat curry for breakfast. While this isn't everyone's cup of chai, knowledge of the disease-fighting power of this scrumptious concoction may have you rethinking your reluctance. Alongside the health benefits, the experience of cooking this curry is a joy in itself.

2 tablespoons extra virgin coconut oil

1 onion, cut into strips

2 garlic cloves, crushed

2 teaspoons freshly grated ginger

2 teaspoons cumin seeds

2 teaspoons ground coriander

1 tablespoon curry powder

1/2 teaspoon ground cinnamon

2 teaspoons ground turmeric

150 g (5 1/2 oz/2 cups) peeled and diced pumpkin (winter squash)

100 ml (3 1/2 fl oz) vegetable stock

600 ml (21 fl oz) additive-free coconut milk

6 drops stevia liquid

160 g (5 3/4 oz/1 cup) almonds

Celtic sea salt and freshly ground black pepper, to season

coriander (cilantro) leaves, to serve

steamed brown rice, to serve

Heat the coconut oil in a large frying pan over medium heat and cook the onion, garlic and ginger for about 5 minutes, or until the onion is translucent. Clear half the pan and add the cumin, coriander, curry powder, cinnamon and turmeric and cook for a couple of minutes, stirring constantly, then combine with the onion mixture. Add the pumpkin and stir-fry for 3–5 minutes, then add the stock, coconut milk and stevia. Stir well to combine and increase the heat to bring it to the boil. Add the almonds, season with salt and pepper and cook for a further 15 minutes.

Serve with the coriander and brown rice.

Health Benefits

Turmeric is a spice consumed daily throughout India. The active ingredient, curcumin, contains potent anti-inflammatory and antioxidant properties linked to the prevention of degenerative disease. It has been reported to have great benefits for people with auto-immune diseases, as it lowers inflammation levels.

CARAMELISED ONION TART

●WF ●DF ●GF ●VEG ●VG   SERVES 8

This lovely and impressive tart has the wow factor, and will most certainly guarantee an abundance of guinea pigs lining up to give it a thumbs-up. The filling fusion of sweetness, tartness and savoury flavours gives it a memorable taste that lingers long after your last bite.

CASHEW CREAM

120 g (4¼ oz/¾ cup) raw unsalted cashews

2 garlic cloves

Celtic sea salt

1 tablespoon freshly squeezed lemon juice

PIE FILLING

60 ml (2 fl oz/¼ cup) cold-pressed extra
  virgin olive oil

4 large brown onions, thinly sliced

Celtic sea salt

freshly ground black pepper

1 tablespoon rice malt syrup

1½ cups English spinach and kale
  leaves, sliced

1 tablespoon apple cider vinegar

TART CRUST

150 g (5½ oz/1½ cups) almond meal

½ teaspoon Celtic sea salt

1 teaspoon bicarbonate of soda
  (baking soda)

½ teaspoon dried rosemary

60 ml (2 fl oz/¼ cup) cold-pressed extra
  virgin olive oil

Preheat the oven to 180°C (350°F/Gas 4) and lightly grease a 22 cm (8½ inch) pie dish.

To make the cashew cream, place the cashews, garlic, salt and lemon juice in a food processor with 60 ml (2 fl oz/¼ cup) of filtered water and process until thick and creamy. Add more water if required.

To make the filling, heat the olive oil in a large frying pan over low heat and cook the onion, salt, pepper and rice malt syrup for about 30 minutes, or until the onion is caramelised. Add the spinach and kale and cook for a further 10 minutes, or until tender. Drain off any excess liquid and add the apple cider vinegar.

To make the pastry, combine the almond meal, salt, bicarbonate of soda and rosemary in a large bowl and stir to combine.

In a separate bowl, whisk the olive oil with 1 tablespoon of cold filtered water. Stir the olive oil and water into the dry ingredients and mix well to combine.

Spoon the mixture into the prepared pie dish and spread evenly over the base and up the sides, removing any excess pastry. Pop in the oven and bake for 10 minutes.

Remove from the oven and allow to cool slightly before adding the cashew cream and then the onion mixture. Return to the oven and bake for a further 15 minutes, or until the crust is golden.

FRIDAY NIGHT PIZZA

● WF   ● GF   ● SF   ● VEG   MAKES ONE 30 CM (12 INCH) PIZZA

This pizza is the perfect indulgence, without the guilt. There are two options for bases to choose from — both deliver all the satisfaction of a regular pizza, but without the gnawing tummy pain that accompanies gluten-filled crusts. Quick and easy to make, the bases are crisp, yet soft and light with a subtle texture, and the herbs and spices add an extra flavour boost.

To veganise: Swap out the spinach base for a cauliflower base (below) and omit the goat's cheese and replace with 3 tablespoons Basil Pesto (see page 194).

3 tablespoons tomato paste
  (concentrated purée)

60 g (2^1/$_4$ oz/^{1}/$_2$ cup) crumbled goat's cheese

4 tomatoes, thinly sliced

nutritional yeast flakes, to serve

SPINACH BASE

cold-pressed extra virgin olive oil,
  for greasing

1 cup English spinach leaves

1 organic egg, whisked

100 g (3^1/$_2$ oz/1 cup) grated cheddar cheese

1 teaspoon dried basil

^{1}/$_2$ teaspoon oregano

Celtic sea salt

freshly ground black pepper

CAULIFLOWER BASE

cold-pressed extra virgin olive oil,
  for greasing

1 tablespoon chia seeds

1 cup cooked, shredded cauliflower

100 g (3^1/$_2$ oz/1 cup) almond meal

^{1}/$_2$ cup nutritional yeast flakes

1 garlic clove, finely chopped

1^1/$_2$ teaspoons dried Italian herbs

pinch of caraway seeds

To make the spinach base, preheat the oven to 220°C (425°F/Gas 7) and lightly grease a 30 cm (12 inch) pizza tray with olive oil.

Place the spinach leaves in a food processor and pulse.

Place the egg, cheese and herbs in a large bowl and add the spinach. Stir to combine well and season with salt and pepper to taste.

Spread the dough evenly onto the prepared pizza tray and bake in the oven for 12–15 minutes, or until the edges begin to brown.

Remove from the oven and set the grill (broiler) to high. Top the base with the tomato paste, goat's cheese and tomato slices and grill for 2–3 minutes. Sprinkle with nutritional yeast flakes and serve.

If you are using the cauliflower base, preheat the oven to 230°C (450°F/Gas 8) and lightly grease a 30 cm (12 inch) pizza tray with olive oil.

Place the chia seeds and 60 ml (2 fl oz/^{1}/$_4$ cup) of water in a bowl and set aside for 15 minutes.

Add the soaked chia seeds to a large bowl with all the other ingredients and mix well.

Spread the dough evenly onto the prepared pizza tray and bake in the oven for 12–15 minutes, or until the edges begin to brown.

Remove from the oven and set aside to cool. Preheat the grill (broiler) to high. Top the base with the tomato paste, goat's cheese and tomato slices and grill for 5 minutes. Sprinkle with nutritional yeast flakes and serve.

LENTIL MOUSSAKA

WF DF GF SF VEG VG   SERVES 3–4

When prepared with love and flavour, the humble lentil comes into its own. This moussaka is completely free of all forms of stodge.

1 eggplant (aubergine), sliced

2–3 zucchini (courgettes), sliced

Celtic sea salt

60 ml (2 fl oz/¼ cup) cold-pressed extra virgin olive oil

2 garlic cloves, minced

1 onion, sliced

1 shallot, chopped

2 tablespoons apple cider vinegar

2 x 400 g (14 oz) tins diced tomatoes

2 x 400 g (14 oz) tins lentils, drained

125 ml (4 fl oz/½ cup) vegetable stock

2 teaspoons oregano leaves

½ teaspoon ground cinnamon

2 tablespoons nutritional yeast flakes

SUNFLOWER SEED CHEESE

145 g (5 oz/1 cup) sunflower seeds, soaked in water for 3 hours

2 garlic cloves

juice of ½ lemon

3 tablespoons nutritional yeast flakes

pinch of Celtic sea salt

120 ml (3¾ fl oz) filtered water

Preheat the oven to 200°C (400°F/Gas 6).

Place the eggplant and zucchini in a colander and sprinkle with salt. Set aside for 30 minutes then rinse off the salt.

Put the eggplant and zucchini on a baking tray and brush with 2 tablespoons of the olive oil then bake in the oven for 20 minutes, or until browned.

Remove from the oven and increase the oven temperature to 220°C (425°F/Gas 7).

Meanwhile, make the sauce. Add the remaining olive oil to a large saucepan over medium heat and sauté the garlic, onion and shallot for 5 minutes, or until browned. Add the apple cider vinegar, tomatoes, lentils, stock, oregano and cinnamon and season to taste. Cover, reduce the heat and simmer over medium–low for about 15 minutes.

To make the sunflower seed cheese, place all the ingredients in a food processor and blend until smooth. If you'd like a creamier cheese, add some filtered water to the mix. Place in the refrigerator for 30 minutes to firm up.

To assemble the moussaka, place a layer of the cooked eggplant and zucchini in a 28 x 18 x 5 cm (11¼ x 7 x 2 inch) baking dish. Pour a layer of sauce over the vegetables, and then repeat. Top with the sunflower seed cheese and scatter over the nutritional yeast flakes. Bake in the oven for 15–20 minutes or until the top is crispy.

BEAUTIFUL BEETROOT BOURGUIGNON

WF DF GF SF VEG VG   SERVES 4

A vegetarian interpretation of the classic bourguignon: rustic, robust and oozing with flavour. This is a fantastic make-ahead meal for any night of the week and, although it's perfectly suited to winter, it can be adapted to fit into any season.

2 tablespoons cold-pressed extra virgin olive oil

1 brown onion, chopped

4 garlic cloves, minced

1 red capsicum (pepper), seeds and membrane removed, chopped

1 cup mushrooms, sliced

8 small beetroot (beets), peeled and quartered

4 carrots, chopped

2 thyme sprigs

Celtic sea salt

freshly ground black pepper, to taste

2 tablespoons tomato paste (concentrated purée)

60 ml (2 fl oz/¼ cup) apple cider vinegar

500 ml (17 fl oz/2 cups) vegetable stock

2 tablespoons freshly squeezed lemon juice

1 teaspoon grated lemon zest

Cauliflower Mash, to serve (see page 157)

Heat the olive oil in a large heavy-based saucepan over medium heat. Add the onion, garlic, capsicum and mushrooms and sauté for 7–10 minutes, or until the vegetables soften.

Add the beetroot, carrot, thyme, salt and pepper to the pan and cook, stirring occasionally, for 5 minutes. Add the tomato paste, apple cider vinegar, stock, lemon juice and zest and reduce the heat to low. Simmer for 35–40 minutes.

Serve with Cauliflower Mash.

QUINOA RISOTTO WITH PUMPKIN AND SPINACH

●WF ●DF ●GF ●SF ●VEG ●VG   SERVES 2

Unfortunately with the renowned Italian risotto comes the health downfalls of refined, white rice. But there's no need to regret the dismissal of this unclassy grain — quinoa is a classic swap that will absorb flavours beautifully, just as an authentic risotto should.

1/2 **small butternut pumpkin (squash), peeled and cut into 2.5 cm (1 inch) pieces**

2–3 tablespoons cold-pressed extra virgin olive oil

1 brown onion, chopped

4 garlic cloves, minced

200 g (7 oz/1 cup) quinoa, rinsed

750 ml (26 fl oz/3 cups) vegetable stock or water

400 g (14 oz) tin diced tomatoes

1 tablespoon freshly chopped herbs, such as rosemary, oregano, thyme

1/2 **teaspoon Celtic sea salt**

freshly ground black pepper

1 tablespoon grated lemon zest

2 tablespoons freshly squeezed lemon juice

1 tablespoon apple cider vinegar

150 g (51/2 oz) baby English spinach leaves

4 tablespoons nutritional yeast flakes

Preheat the oven to 200°C (400°F/Gas 6).

Place the pumpkin on a baking tray and roast for 30 minutes.

Meanwhile, make the risotto. Heat the olive oil in a large saucepan over medium–high heat and sauté the onion and garlic for 5 minutes or until translucent, stirring often. Clear one side of the pan and add the quinoa. Stir for 1 minute, until it is slightly crispy, then stir to combine with the onion.

Increase the heat and add the stock or water over the next 10 minutes, 1 ladleful at a time, letting each ladleful of stock be absorbed before adding more, and stirring constantly.

Add the tomatoes, herbs and seasonings, lemon zest and juice and apple cider vinegar and cook for a further 10 minutes, until the quinoa is tender but still slightly *al dente*. Add the spinach and roasted pumpkin and cook for a further 5 minutes.

Remove from the heat and stir through the yeast flakes.

⤳ Supercharged Tip ⤳

I love to serve this in shallow, earthenware bowls garnished with extra yeast flakes.

BLACK BEAN BURGERS WITH GREEN SALAD

●WF ●DF ●GF ●SF ●VEG ●VG   SERVES 2

The black bean is a clever little morsel. Unlike other beans, it holds within its glossy skin a matchless balance of both protein and fibre. These burgers will satisfy you for hours, while keeping your digestive system moving smoothly.

75 g (2 1/2 oz/1/2 cup) sunflower seeds

75 g (2 1/2 oz/1/2 cup) pepitas (pumpkin seeds)

1 carrot, grated

400 g (14 oz) tin black beans, rinsed and drained

1 onion, chopped

1 teaspoon ground cinnamon

1 teaspoon cumin

1 teaspoon ground coriander

1/2 chilli, chopped

1/2 teaspoon cayenne pepper

2 tablespoons cold-pressed extra virgin olive oil

Celtic sea salt and freshly ground black pepper

SALAD

1 cup English spinach leaves

1 cup mixed basil and mint leaves

1 cucumber, sliced

1 green capsicum (pepper), seeds and membrane removed, chopped

DRESSING

2 tablespoons cold-pressed extra virgin olive oil

3 teaspoons freshly squeezed lemon juice

Preheat the oven to 200°C (400°F/Gas 6) and lightly grease a baking tray.

Place the seeds in a food processor and grind until coarsely chopped. Add the carrot to the food processor and mix for 10 seconds. Add three quarters of the black beans, the onion, spices, olive oil and salt and pepper and then mix again for 10 seconds.

Add the remaining beans to the mixture. Use your hands to form small patties and place them on the baking tray.

Bake in the oven for about 20 minutes.

Meanwhile, to make the salad, mix all the ingredients in a bowl. To make the dressing, whisk the olive oil and lemon juice together.

Serve the patties with the dressed salad on the side.

EASY PEASY BROWN FRIED RICE

◆ WF ◆ DF ◆ GF ◆ SF ◆ VEG   SERVES 4

For those times when you have leftover brown rice stored away in the back of the fridge, this potluck recipe will be your perfect lazy-night meal. It's far tastier than a Chinese take-out variety. Exert minimal effort, with maximum delectability.

To veganise: Replace the eggs with ½ cup pumpkin purée.

1 tablespoon extra virgin coconut oil

2 shallots, finely diced

2 garlic cloves, crushed

1 red capsicum (pepper), seeds and
   membrane removed, chopped

50 g (1¾ oz) peas, fresh or frozen

40 g (1½ oz/⅓ cup) green beans, sliced
   into 2 cm (¾ inch) pieces

1 carrot, finely diced

925 g (2 lb 1 oz/5 cups) cooked brown rice

2 tablespoons wheat-free tamari

2 organic eggs, lightly beaten

Heat the coconut oil in a large frying pan over high heat until it sizzles. Add the shallots, garlic, capsicum, peas, beans and carrot and cook, stirring, for 10 minutes or until lightly cooked. Add the rice and cook for 5 minutes, stirring occasionally. Add the tamari and cook, stirring, for 2 minutes.

Clear one side of the pan and pour in the egg. Cook for 30 seconds and then scramble with a fork and combine it with the rest of the ingredients.

It's that easy.

FRENCH ROASTED RATATOUILLE

WF DF GF SF VEG VG   SERVES 4

This 'touille is a great way to empty the fridge. Serve it as a chopping-board meal with a side of Green Beans and Spinach on page 212 and Tuscan Kaleslaw on page 95.

1 eggplant (aubergine), cut into 2.5 cm (1 inch) chunks

1 teaspoon Celtic sea salt

1 sweet potato, cut into 2.5 cm (1 inch) chunks

1 green capsicum (pepper), seeds and membrane removed, chopped

1 brown onion, thickly sliced

2 zucchini (courgettes), cut into 2.5 cm (1 inch) chunks

400 g (14 oz) tin whole peeled tomatoes

DRESSING

$1/2$ teaspoon Celtic sea salt

60 ml (2 fl oz/$1/4$ cup) cold-pressed extra virgin olive oil

4 garlic cloves, finely chopped

2 tablespoons herbes de Provence

$1/4$ teaspoon chilli flakes

2 tablespoons apple cider vinegar

1 tablespoon wheat-free tamari

6 drops stevia liquid (optional)

freshly ground black pepper, to taste

HERBES DE PROVENCE

3 tablespoons dried marjoram

3 tablespoons dried thyme

1 tablespoon dried mint

1 teaspoon dried basil

1 teaspoon dried rosemary

$1/2$ teaspoon dried sage

$1/2$ teaspoon fennel seeds

Preheat the oven to 220°C (425°F/Gas 7).

To make the *herbes de Provence*, place the herbs in a bowl and mix well. Set aside.

Place the eggplant in a bowl, sprinkle with the salt and set aside for 30 minutes.

Remove the eggplant from the bowl and pat dry with paper towel. Add it to a large bowl with the sweet potato, capsicum, onion and zucchini.

To make the dressing, place the salt, olive oil, garlic, *herbes de Provence*, chilli flakes, apple cider vinegar, tamari, stevia and pepper in a glass jar and shake to combine well.

Pour the dressing over the vegetables and toss to ensure they are evenly coated. Spread the vegetables onto a baking tray in a single layer and roast in the oven for 30 minutes.

Meanwhile, warm the tomatoes in a saucepan over medium heat for 7–10 minutes.

Remove the 'touille vegetables from the oven and spoon the tomatoes over the top, letting the sauce cover the roasted vegetables.

Serve warm.

NOTE: Any leftover *herbes de Provence* can be stored in a sealed jar in a cool, dark place for up to 4 months.

MARRAKESH CASSEROLE

🍂 WF   🥛 DF   🌾 GF   🌱 VEG   🌿 VG   SERVES 4

This dish showcases the kaleidoscopic colour and exquisiteness of Moroccan cuisine. It's deliciously rich and heavily spiced, but not overpoweringly hot.

60 ml (2 fl oz/1/4 cup) cold-pressed extra virgin olive oil

1 large onion, roughly chopped

3 garlic cloves, minced

2 cm (3/4 inch) piece of ginger, minced

1 tablespoon ground cinnamon

1 teaspoon cumin

1 tablespoon turmeric

1/4 teaspoon Celtic sea salt

2–3 teaspoons dried harissa

400 g (14 oz) tin diced tomatoes

1 tablespoon rice malt syrup

juice of 1 lemon

1/4 cup coriander (cilantro) leaves

1/4 cup chopped mint leaves

1 small pumpkin (winter squash), peeled and cut into 5 cm (2 inch) pieces

1 sweet potato, peeled and cut into 5 cm (2 inch) pieces

3 carrots, peeled and cut into 5 cm (2 inch) pieces

1 zucchini (courgette), cut into 5 cm (2 inch) pieces

400 g (14 oz) tin chickpeas

cooked quinoa, to serve

coriander (cilantro) sprigs, to serve

1 tablespoon grated lemon zest, to serve

mint leaves, to serve

80 g (23/4 oz/1/2 cup) dry-roasted almonds, to serve

Heat the olive oil in a flame-proof tagine pot or casserole dish over medium heat and sauté the onion for 5 minutes, or until translucent. Add the garlic, ginger and spices and stir well to combine. Add the harissa, tomatoes, rice malt syrup, lemon juice, coriander and mint, bring to the boil and then reduce the heat. Add the pumpkin, sweet potato, carrot and zucchini, stir well so they are all well covered in the sauce and simmer, covered, for 1 hour.

Add the chickpeas and cook for a further 5 minutes.

Serve on a bed of quinoa topped with the coriander, lemon zest, mint and roasted almonds.

EGGPLANT AND GREEN BEAN CURRY

● WF ● DF ● GF ● SF ● VEG ● VG   SERVES 4

There's nothing quite as disappointing as an undercooked eggplant, but the soft creaminess of a perfectly cooked eggplant is the epitome of culinary perfection. Slowly simmered and intermingled with sizzling spices, this curry will whisk you away to eggplant heaven.

4 tablespoons extra virgin coconut oil

6 small eggplants (aubergines), cut into 6 cm (2 1/2 inch) wedges

300 ml (10 1/2 fl oz) tomato passata (puréed tomatoes)

270 ml (9 1/2 fl oz) additive-free coconut milk

300 g (10 1/2 oz) green beans

Celtic sea salt

freshly ground black pepper

80 g (2 3/4 oz/1/2 cup) activated almonds, roughly chopped, to serve

handful of coriander (cilantro) leaves, chopped, to serve

juice of 1 lime

lime halves, to serve

CURRY PASTE

1 large brown onion, chopped

3 garlic cloves, chopped

2 thumb-sized pieces of ginger, chopped

1 large red chilli, finely chopped

1 teaspoon ground cumin

1 teaspoon ground coriander

1 teaspoon cardamom

1 teaspoon turmeric

1 teaspoon curry powder

Place all the curry paste ingredients in a food processor with 2 tablespoons of filtered water and whizz together for a few seconds.

Heat 2 tablespoons of the coconut oil in a large frying pan over medium–high heat and fry the eggplants until browned. Remove from the pan and set aside on paper towel to drain.

Heat the remaining coconut oil in the pan and cook the curry paste ingredients for about 3 minutes. Add the eggplant and stir so it is well covered in the paste. Add the tomato passata and coconut milk and simmer, partially covered, for 10 minutes. Lastly, add the green beans and cook for a further 6 minutes.

Season with salt and pepper, add the almonds, coriander and lime juice and serve with the lime halves on the side.

DAIKON RAVIOLI WITH SUNFLOWER SEED CHEESE AND SUN-DRIED TOMATO SAUCE

WF DF GF SF VEG VG   SERVES 2

Not blessed with supermodel looks, but full of potential, daikon is an Asian superfood that is low in kilojoules and full of vitamin C, phosphorus, potassium and precious digestive enzymes. There is a wealth of health to be enjoyed if you give daikon a chance.

juice of 1 lemon

1 large daikon, thinly sliced into circles

1/2 teaspoon Celtic sea salt

salad leaves, to serve

Sunflower Seed Cheese, see page 123

2 tablespoons olive oil, for drizzling

Celtic sea salt

freshly ground black pepper

SUN-DRIED TOMATO SAUCE

2 tablespoons nutritional yeast flakes

200 g (7 oz) jar sun-dried tomatoes in olive oil, undrained

handful of basil

2 garlic cloves, minced

Place the lemon juice in a large bowl with 500 ml (17 fl oz/2 cups) of warm filtered water. Add the daikon, sprinkle with the salt and soak for 20 minutes.

Drain the water, pat the daikon dry using paper towel and set aside.

To make the sun-dried tomato sauce, place all the ingredients in a food processor and blend until the texture is smooth, adding more olive oil to reach the desired consistency if necessary.

To serve, place your salad leaves on a platter and top with the daikon ravioli, sandwiched with sunflower seed cheese. Spoon over the sun-dried tomato sauce, drizzle with olive oil and season with salt and pepper to taste.

LENTIL PIE WITH CAULIFLOWER MASH

● WF　● DF　● GF　● SF　● VEG　● VG　　SERVES 2

In this hearty dish I've replaced minced meat with lentils. They might be small, but nutritionally they're giants; containing a brilliant source of folate, iron, B vitamins, magnesium and plant protein. They're also a powerful cholesterol fighter due to their high levels of fibre, and have been found to stabilise blood sugar levels and lower the risk of heart disease.

2 tablespoons cold-pressed extra virgin olive oil

1 onion, finely chopped

2 celery stalks, chopped

1 carrot, chopped

1 red capsicum (pepper), seeds and membrane removed, chopped

2 garlic cloves, crushed

400 g (14 oz) tin diced tomatoes

120 ml (4 fl oz) tomato passata (puréed tomatoes)

2 teaspoons chopped thyme

125 ml (4 fl oz/1/2 cup) vegetable stock

400 g (14 oz) tin lentils, rinsed and drained

pinch of Celtic sea salt

freshly ground black pepper, to taste

CAULIFLOWER MASH

1 cauliflower, chopped into florets

125 ml (4 fl oz/1/2 cup) almond milk

3 teaspoons cold-pressed extra virgin olive oil

2 tablespoons nutritional yeast flakes

Preheat the oven to 220°C (425°F/Gas 7).

Heat the olive oil in a medium saucepan over medium heat and sauté the onion for 5 minutes, or until translucent. Add the celery, carrot, capsicum and garlic and cook, stirring, for 2 minutes. Add the tomatoes, tomato passata, thyme, stock and lentils and reduce the heat to low. Simmer for 15 minutes then season with salt and pepper.

To make the mash, line a bamboo steamer with baking paper and steam the cauliflower over a saucepan of gently simmering water for 10 minutes, or until soft. Transfer to a blender and add the almond milk and olive oil then whizz for a few minutes.

To assemble the pie, place the lentil mixture in a pie dish, top with the cauliflower mash and sprinkle with the nutritional yeast flakes. Bake in the oven for 15 minutes.

SUNFLOWER SEED FALAFEL BALLS WITH TAHINI DIPPING SAUCE

●WF ●DF ●GF ●SF ●VEG ●VG   MAKES 4–5

Unfortunately, the kebab-shop versions of these popular little plant-based pleasures are full of refined wheat and fried in cheap seed oils. Cook them at home to ensure an array of healthy ingredients in every bite with these sunflower seed and cashew-based delights.

75 g (2¹/₂ oz/¹/₂ cup) sunflower seeds

80 g (2³/₄ oz/¹/₂ cup) cashews

1 tablespoon organic nut butter, softened

2 tablespoons basil leaves, chopped

¹/₂ teaspoon ground cumin

2 tablespoons freshly squeezed lemon juice

1 teaspoon chopped coriander (cilantro) leaves

2 tablespoons chopped red capsicum (pepper)

1 garlic clove, minced

¹/₄ shallot, chopped

pinch of Celtic sea salt

40 g (1¹/₂ oz/¹/₄ cup) toasted sesame seeds, for coating

lettuce leaf, to serve

TAHINI DIPPING SAUCE

3 tablespoons tahini

6 drops stevia liquid

2 tablespoons freshly squeezed lemon juice

pinch of Celtic sea salt

Preheat the oven to 220°C (425°F/Gas 7) and line a baking tray with baking paper.

To make the tahini dipping sauce, place all the ingredients in a food processor with 2 tablespoons of filtered water and blend until smooth and creamy.

Place all the falafel ingredients, except the sesame seeds and lettuce, in a food processor and pulse until thoroughly blended.

Use an ice-cream scoop to form round balls. Roll in the sesame seeds, transfer to the baking tray and bake for 20 minutes, or until crispy.

Serve in a lettuce leaf and dress with the tahini dipping sauce.

DESSERTS

There'll be no more skipping dessert, and that's final. Whatever you're craving, sweet treats don't have to be off limits, especially when they've been tweaked to include plenty of deliciously nourishing and nutritionally beneficial veg to linger softly and sweetly on your palate long after the meal is over. Indulge yourself with creative confectionery and make some love heart chocolates, get stuck into a triple mint slice or a slice of gooey chocolate cake, or hatch a simple batch of spinach ice cream. Pass the spoon.

LOVE HEART CHOCOLATES

● WF ● DF ● GF ● SF ● VEG ● VG   SERVES 2

It surprises me that people still choose to frequent confectionery aisles, when the superiority of homemade chocolate is so simple to achieve. Whether you're indulging in a little self-love, or wanting to impress that special someone, these creations exude adoration.

DARK CHOCOLATE

40 g (1¹/₂ oz) shaved cacao butter

¹/₄ cup organic coconut butter

30 g (1 oz/¹/₄ cup) raw cacao powder

3 tablespoons extra virgin coconut oil

1 tablespoon alcohol-free vanilla extract

10–12 drops stevia liquid, or 1 teaspoon powdered, or to taste

To make the dark chocolate, melt the butters in a bowl over a saucepan of boiling water. Add the other ingredients and whisk until smooth.

Place in love heart moulds and freeze for 30 minutes.

Remove from the freezer and wait a few minutes before popping the chocolate out from the moulds. If in hard moulds, tap the bottom until the hearts fall out.

To make white chocolate, follow the method above but omit the cacao powder.

The chocolates will keep in the freezer for up to 1 month.

⤳ Supercharged Tip ⤳

You can make other versions to suit your taste by adding orange or peppermint extract, crushed raw almonds, walnuts or cashews.

CHOCOLATE AND COCONUT ROUGHS

WF DF GF SF VEG VG   MAKES 6

These coconut roughs are a truly healthy answer to your confectionery cravings.

70 g (2¹/₂ oz/1¹/₄ cups) unsweetened
   coconut flakes

65 g (2¹/₄ oz/¹/₂ cup) slivered almonds

140 g (5 oz/²/₃ cup) organic nut butter

40 g (1¹/₂ oz/¹/₃ cup) organic coconut butter

³/₄ teaspoon stevia powder

¹/₂ teaspoon alcohol-free vanilla extract

1 tablespoon raw cacao powder

2 tablespoons raw cacao nibs

Line a 6-hole (250 ml/9 fl oz/1 cup) capacity muffin tin with paper liners.

Place the coconut flakes and almonds in a large bowl.

Place the nut and coconut butters in a bowl over a saucepan of gently simmering water until melted. Add the stevia, vanilla extract, cacao powder and nibs, stirring frequently until well combined. Remove from the heat and pour the mixture over the coconut flakes and almonds, stirring well so they are well coated.

Divide the mixture evenly among the muffin holes and pop in the fridge for 1 hour, or until set.

The roughs will keep in a sealed container in the fridge for up to 1 week.

CRUNCHY CHOCOLATE BUCKWHEAT BARS

WF GF VEG   MAKES 12

My friend Alexx from alexxstuart.com has created this beautiful recipe.

65 g (2¹/₄ oz/1 cup) additive-free
   shredded coconut

1 tablespoon raw cacao powder

75 g (2¹/₂ oz/¹/₂ cup) pepitas (pumpkin seeds)

125 ml (4 fl oz/¹/₂ cup) coconut oil

125–170 ml (4–5¹/₂ fl oz/¹/₂–²/₃ cup) rice
   malt syrup

120 g (4¹/₄ oz/1 cup) tapioca flour

1 organic egg

160 g (5³/₄ oz/1 cup) buckwheat 'buckinis'

120 g (4¹/₄ oz) 85% dark chocolate, for
   melting and drizzling (optional)

Preheat the oven to 180°C (350°F/Gas 4) and line a baking tray with baking paper.

Place all the ingredients, except the buckinis and dark chocolate, in a food processor and pulse until well mixed. Add the buckinis and pulse a few more times.

Spread the mixture evenly and firmly over the prepared baking tray and bake for 20–25 minutes.

Remove from the oven and make indents into the mixture marking out your 12 bars.

Cool on a wire rack, and when cool, cut completely into 12 bars. Drizzle over the melted chocolate before serving.

FRESH BLUEBERRY FUDGE

●WF ●DF ●GF ●VEG ●VG   SERVES 2

It's hip to be square. Make a colourful statement with this special-occasion blueberry fudge — it's the ultimate healthy sweet-tooth fix.

155 g (5¹/2 oz/1 cup) raw cashews

55 g (2 oz/1 cup) unsweetened coconut flakes, plus 2 tablespoons, for decorating

1 tablespoon extra virgin coconut oil

2 teaspoons alcohol-free vanilla extract

80 ml (2¹/2 fl oz/¹/3 cup) rice malt syrup

155 g (5¹/2 oz/1 cup) fresh blueberries

Place the cashews in a bowl, cover with filtered water and soak for 2 hours. Drain.

Drain the cashews and place them in a food processor with the coconut flakes. Whizz until the texture is smooth. Add the remaining ingredients and whizz again until combined.

Line a 20 x 10 cm (8 x 4 inch) baking tray with baking paper. Press the fudge into the baking tray, sprinkle with 2 tablespoons of coconut flakes and place in the freezer for 3 hours, or until set.

Remove from the freezer and cut into squares.

The fudge will keep in an airtight container in the fridge for up to 3 days, or for a week in the freezer.

HAZELNUT, CHOCOLATE AND BERRY PUDDING

●WF ●DF ●GF ●VEG ●VG   SERVES 3

Gee whizz. This recipe has only three steps. Whizz, chill and scatter. It's funny what emerges when you combine hazelnuts, avocado, berries and cacao. Enter a spankingly delicious pud that'll rock the socks off any pudding seen sitting around in coffee shops and cake stalls, whispering in honeyed tones, inviting you in, but then leaving you and your gurgling stomach with discomforting memories and promises of never again.

2 avocados, peeled, stones removed and cubed

1 cup mixed berries

55 g (2 oz) organic hazelnut butter

40 g (1½ oz/¼ cup) hazelnuts

55 g (2 oz/½ cup) raw cacao powder

6 drops stevia liquid, or 2 tablespoons xylitol or sweetener of your choice

125 ml (4 fl oz/½ cup) coconut water (see note)

unsweetened coconut flakes and fresh berries, to serve

Place all the ingredients in a food processor and whizz until smooth.

Transfer to a bowl and chill in the fridge for 20 minutes.

Scatter with the coconut flakes and fresh berries and serve cold. The pudding will keep in an airtight container in the fridge for up to 4 days.

NOTE: For a creamier consistency, substitute the coconut water with the same quantity of coconut milk.

MIXED BERRY COBBLER

●WF ●GF ●VEG   SERVES 5—6

There aren't many things as comforting as the biscuity crumbly top and deliciously sweet berries of a cobbler. This is one of Alexx Stuart's yummy recipes — she's my go-to dessert-maker. Her number one tip for the best cobbler in town is to place it in the fridge before baking. This will create the chilled pastry nuggets that are essential for the perfect biscuity cobbler result. See page 171 for a vegan-friendly Berry Crumble.

FILLING

600 g (1 lb 5 oz) mixed berries

80 ml (2½ fl oz/⅓ cup) rice malt syrup

½ teaspoon vanilla bean powder

1 heaped tablespoon tapioca flour

zest of 1 lime

PASTRY

50 g (1¾ oz/½ cup) almond meal

120 g (4¼ oz/1 cup) tapioca flour

pinch of Celtic sea salt

1 teaspoon gluten-free baking powder

80 g (2¾ oz) chilled organic butter, cut into cubes

1 organic egg, whisked

½ teaspoon vanilla bean powder

½ teaspoon ground cinnamon, for sprinkling (optional)

1–2 tablespoons coconut sugar, for sprinkling (optional)

Preheat the oven to 200°C (400°F/Gas 6).

To make the filling, combine all the ingredients in a bowl and stir to mix.

Pour into a 20 cm (8 inch) pie dish.

To make the pastry, place the almond meal, tapioca flour, salt and baking powder in a food processor and pulse for 2 seconds to combine. Add the chilled butter and pulse twice to create a sandy texture.

Whisk the egg and vanilla together, pour half the mixture into the food processor and pulse to bring the pastry together. If the pastry hasn't started to form lumps, add a touch more egg mixture and pulse for a further few seconds.

Turn the pastry out onto a clean work surface and wrap it in baking paper. Place in the fridge for 20 minutes to chill (this is the step that makes it oh-so-deliciously-crumbly).

Break the pastry into small chunks and use it to cover the filling. It doesn't matter if the cobbler isn't entirely covered.

Sprinkle over the cinnamon and coconut sugar, if using, and bake in the oven for 35–40 minutes, or until the top is golden brown.

This is delicious served with Coconut Icing (see page 182).

NOTE: Use any leftover egg mixture in a cake or muffin batter.

BERRY CRUMBLE

◆ WF ◗ DF ♥ GF ◆ VEG ♥ VG   SERVES 5—6

This recipe reminds me of a friend's mum, Elizabeth, who worked as a waitress at a famous restaurant. One night she was standing in the kitchen waiting to take out desserts and the chef yelled at her 'Elizabeth! Crumble!' She obeyed and crumbled onto the floor. Berry Crumble is something that you can serve any time of the day. I love this crumbly piece of heaven best when served warm alongside coconut ice cream, with no loud chefs in sight.

TOPPING

160 g (5³/4 oz/1 cup) almonds,
  roughly chopped

75 g (2¹/2 oz/¹/2 cup) pepitas
  (pumpkin seeds)

75 g (2¹/2 oz/¹/2 cup) sunflower seeds

55 g (2 oz/1 cup) unsweetened
  coconut flakes

75 g (2¹/2 oz/¹/2 cup) hazelnuts

2 tablespoons extra virgin coconut oil

2 tablespoons rice malt syrup

FILLING

60 ml (2 fl oz/¹/4 cup) rice malt syrup

1 teaspoon vanilla bean powder, or one
  scraped out vanilla pod

1 tablespoon tapioca flour

zest of 1 lime

600 g (1 lb 5 oz) mixed berries (see note)

Preheat the oven to 180°C (350°F/Gas 4) and line a baking tray with baking paper.

Place all the topping ingredients in a bowl and use your hands to combine well, ensuring all the ingredients are well coated.

Transfer the mixture to the prepared baking tray and bake for 15–20 minutes.

Remove and set aside to cool – it will get its crunch once it cools down.

To make the filling, mix the rice malt syrup, vanilla and tapioca flour with the lime zest.

Place the berries in a saucepan and pour over the syrup. Mix gently to combine, taking care not to break up the berries. Cook them over medium heat for 15 minutes.

Transfer to a 20 cm (8 inch) pie dish and sprinkle over the topping ingredients. Serve warm or cold.

This will keep in the fridge in an airtight container for up to 5 days.

NOTE: If berries aren't in season, try substituting the same quantity of other fruits.

⤙Supercharged Tip⤚

Add a tablespoon of raw cacao or maca powder to the topping as it comes out of the oven. It will give you a delicious malty chocolate taste and enhance the flavours.

CAULIFLOWER AND RASPBERRY CHEESECAKE

⬤ WF ⬤ DF ⬤ GF ⬤ VEG ⬤ VG   MAKES 1

This unusual combination will surprise you with its silky, sweet enchantment. Creamy cauli and bright pink raspberries are a pleasant pair-up; a perfect use of plant-based produce in delicious dessert form.

BASE

120 g (4$^{1}/_{4}$ oz/$^{3}/_{4}$ cup) raw, unsalted cashews

65 g (2$^{1}/_{4}$ oz/1 cup) additive-free shredded coconut

$^{1}/_{4}$ teaspoon stevia powder

60 ml (2 fl oz/$^{1}/_{4}$ cup) freshly squeezed lemon juice

1 tablespoon melted coconut butter

FILLING

310 g (11 oz/2 cups) raw, unsalted cashews

$^{1}/_{2}$ cup coconut butter

300 g (10$^{1}/_{2}$ oz/1$^{1}/_{2}$ cups) cooked cauliflower (about 1 small)

125 g (4$^{1}/_{2}$ oz/1 cup) frozen raspberries

1 teaspoon alcohol-free vanilla extract

1 tablespoon freshly squeezed lemon juice

1 tablespoon of rice malt syrup, or $^{1}/_{4}$ teaspoon stevia powder

80 ml (2$^{1}/_{2}$ fl oz/$^{1}/_{3}$ cup) additive-free coconut milk

60 g (2$^{1}/_{4}$ oz/$^{1}/_{2}$ cup) fresh raspberries, for decorating

Place the cashews in a bowl, cover with filtered water and soak for 2 hours. Drain.

To make the base, place the cashews and shredded coconut in a food processor and blend until finely chopped. Transfer to a large bowl and stir in the remaining ingredients.

Turn out onto a clean work surface and roll out into a dough. Press the dough evenly into a 16 cm (6$^{1}/_{4}$ inch) cake tin and place in the freezer for 30 minutes.

To make the filling, combine all the ingredients, except the fresh berries, in a food processor and blend until smooth.

Remove the base from the freezer and pour in the filling, using a spatula to smooth it over. Return to the freezer for 30 minutes, or the fridge for 1 hour, until set.

Top with fresh berries and serve.

This will keep for up to 1 week in the fridge, and 2 weeks in the freezer.

LEMON SLICES

● WF ● DF ● GF ● SF ● VEG ● VG   MAKES 12

These darlings will be a complete show-stopper at your next social gathering, and your guests will be pleasantly surprised that this decadent, lemony slice is completely free from sugar, and full of raw phytonutrients.

BASE

120 g (4¼ oz/¾ cup) raw, unsalted cashews

55 g (2 oz/1 cup) additive-free
   shredded coconut

¼ teaspoon stevia powder

60 ml (2 fl oz/¼ cup) freshly squeezed
   lemon juice

1 tablespoon melted coconut butter

FILLING

250 g (9 oz) raw, unsalted cashews

½ cup coconut butter

zest and juice of 2 limes

juice of 2 lemons

1 teaspoon alcohol-free vanilla extract

¼ teaspoon stevia powder

60 ml (2 fl oz/¼ cup) additive-free
   coconut milk

Place the cashews in a bowl, cover with filtered water and soak for 2 hours. Drain.

To make the base, combine the cashews and shredded coconut in a food processor and blend. Stir in the remaining ingredients, adding some filtered water if it looks too dry and won't hold together.

Use your hands to mould the mixture into a dough and then press the dough into a freezer-proof tray. Place in the freezer for 30 minutes.

To make the filling, combine all the ingredients in a food processor and blend until smooth.

Remove the base from the freezer and add the filling, using the back of a spoon to smooth the top.

Return the slice to the fridge for 30 minutes or until set.

Cut into slices and serve.

This will keep in an airtight container in the fridge for up to 1 week, or 2 weeks in the freezer.

GOOEY CHOCOLATE CAKE

WF · GF · SF · VEG   MAKES 1

This chocolate cake deserves a royal procession. Built only of nourishing, vitamin-rich wholefoods, it delivers unbelievable chocolate richness that will bring you to your knees. Crowned with a contrast of beautiful pink raspberries, this gooey delight represents royalty in every bite.

125 g (4¹/₂ oz) organic butter, at room temperature, plus extra, for greasing

200 g (7 oz) xylitol

25 g (1 oz) coconut flour

125 g (4¹/₂ oz/1¹/₄ cups) almond meal

1¹/₂ teaspoons gluten-free baking powder

1 teaspoon bicarbonate of soda (baking soda)

pinch of Celtic sea salt

55 g (2 oz/¹/₂ cup) raw cacao powder

4 organic eggs, lightly beaten

1 teaspoon alcohol-free vanilla extract

3 tablespoons organic butter or light olive oil

2 tablespoons brazil nut and linseed butter, or other nut butter

100 ml (3¹/₂ fl oz) additive-free coconut milk

125 ml (4 fl oz/¹/₂ cup) almond milk

coconut cream and raspberries, for topping

Preheat the oven to 180°C (350°F/Gas 4) and grease a 16 cm (6¹/₄ inch) cake tin.

Use an electric mixer to cream the butter and xylitol.

Add the coconut flour, almond meal, baking powder, bicarbonate of soda, salt and cacao to the bowl.

In a separate bowl, whisk the eggs and vanilla together. Add the butter or oil, brazil nut and linseed butter and coconut milk and stir well to combine.

Slowly add the wet mixture into the dry, finally adding the almond milk.

Spoon the batter into the cake tin and bake for 40–45 minutes.

Remove from the oven and transfer to a wire rack to cool before icing.

Once cool, top with the coconut cream and raspberries.

The cake will keep in an airtight container in the fridge for up to 5 days.

PUMPKIN AND BERRY MUFFINS

WF DF GF VEG   MAKES 18

A guilt-free stud muffin that's a wholesome take on the traditional sugar-laden muffin.
To veganise: Substitute the eggs with 2 tablespoons ground or whole chia or flaxseeds soaked in 120 ml (3¾ fl oz) of water for 15 minutes and add 1 mashed banana.

2 cups steamed and puréed
  pumpkin (winter squash) (about
  ½ uncooked pumpkin)

250 g (9 oz/1 cup) organic nut butter

4 organic eggs

100 g (3½ oz/1 cup) almond meal

2 tablespoons flaxseed meal

2 teaspoons gluten-free baking powder

60 ml (2 fl oz/¼ cup) rice malt syrup or
  ½ teaspoon stevia

125 g (4½ oz/1 cup) frozen berries

Preheat the oven to 160°C (315°F/Gas 2–3) and line 18 holes in two 12-hole 60 ml (2 fl oz/¼ cup) capacity muffin tins with muffin liners.

Place all the ingredients, except the berries, in a food processor and whizz to combine. Stir in the berries.

Divide the mixture evenly among the prepared muffin holes.

Bake in the oven for 25 minutes, or until a skewer inserted into one of the muffins comes out clean.

Remove from the oven and cool on a wire rack.

Stored in the fridge in an airtight container, these muffins will keep for up to 5 days.

BANANA AND QUINOA COOKIES

WF DF GF VEG VG   MAKES 20

A healthy cookie: squidgy, full of sweet flavour and packed with everyday superfoods.

80 g (2¾ oz/½ cup) raw, unsalted cashews

270 g (9½ oz/1 cup) cooked quinoa

1 banana

2 tablespoons coconut flour

60 ml (2 fl oz/¼ cup) almond milk

Place the cashews in a bowl, cover with filtered water and soak for 2 hours. Drain.

Preheat the oven to 220°C (425°F/Gas 7) and line a baking tray with baking paper.

Place all the ingredients in a food processor and blend until smooth.

Use your hands to roll the mixture into balls and place them on the baking tray. Squash them down a little with your hands and bake in the oven for 25 minutes.

Cool on a wire rack. These will keep in an airtight container in the fridge for up to 4 days.

RAW BERRY AND CHOCOLATE TORTE

● WF ● DF ● GF ● VEG   MAKES 1

If you want to make friends, this tantalising torte is a sure-fire way to do it. Who could resist a rich, chocolatey dessert that is completely guilt-free? You and your new best friends will be bursting with bliss after just one bite.

BASE

175 g (6 oz/1^{1}/2 cups) raw walnuts

zest of 1 lemon

^{1}/2 cup dried berries

60 ml (2 fl oz/^{1}/4 cup) melted extra virgin
  coconut oil

1 teaspoon stevia powder

FILLING

155 g (5^{1}/2 oz/1 cup) raw, unsalted cashews

40 g (1^{1}/2 oz/^{1}/3 cup) raw cacao powder

115 g (4 oz) cacao butter, grated and melted

2 tablespoons rice malt syrup, or
  1 teaspoon stevia powder

2 tablespoons additive-free coconut milk

juice of 1 lemon

2 cups mixed berries, plus extra, for
  decorating (optional)

Place the cashews in a bowl, cover with filtered water and soak for 2 hours. Drain.

To make the base, place the walnuts in a food processor and blend until they are finely chopped. Transfer to a bowl and add the lemon zest.

Place the coconut oil and dried berries in the food processor and blend. Add to the walnut mixture and combine well.

Press the mixture into a 20 cm (8 inch) springform cake tin and chill in the freezer for 30 minutes.

To make the filling, place all the ingredients in the food processor and blend until smooth.

Remove the base from the freezer and spoon the filling over the top.

Chill for 2 hours in the fridge, or 1 hour in the freezer, until set. Scatter over the extra berries before serving.

This will keep in an airtight container for up to 1 week in the fridge, or 2 weeks in the freezer.

TRIPLE MINT SLICE

WF · DF · GF · VEG · VG   SERVES 4–6

Enjoying the freshness of mint after a big meal is a smart way to aid digestion, and this triple mint slice is the ultimate way to reap those benefits. Satisfyingly sweet and full of chlorophyll-rich spinach, this delicious treat contains a therapeutic dose of tummy-soothing peppermint extract.

BASE LAYER

120 g (4¼ oz/¾ cup) raw, unsalted cashews

55 g (2 oz/1 cup) additive-free shredded coconut

¼ teaspoon stevia powder

60 ml (2 fl oz/¼ cup) freshly squeezed lemon juice

1 tablespoon melted coconut butter

MINT LAYER

2 cups English spinach leaves

35 g (1¼ oz/¼ cup) coconut butter

2 tablespoons rice malt syrup

235 g (8½ oz/1½ cups) raw, unsalted cashews

pinch of Celtic sea salt

¼ teaspoon alcohol-free peppermint extract

2 teaspoons alcohol-free vanilla extract

CHOCOLATE LAYER

55 g (2 oz/½ cup) raw cacao powder

3 tablespoons extra virgin coconut oil

35 g (1¼ oz/¼ cup) coconut butter

2 tablespoons rice malt syrup

1 teaspoon alcohol-free vanilla extract

Place the cashews in separate bowls, cover with filtered water and soak for 2 hours. Drain.

To make the base, combine the cashews and coconut in a food processor and process until finely chopped. Stir in the remaining ingredients, adding a little filtered water if it looks too dry.

Using your hands, mould into a dough and press into a 16 cm (6¼ inch) springform cake tin.

Place in the freezer for 30 minutes.

Meanwhile, make the other layers. To make the mint layer, combine all the ingredients in a food processor and process until smooth.

To make the chocolate layer, place all the ingredients in a bowl over a saucepan of simmering water and stir until all ingredients have melted together.

To assemble, remove the base from the freezer, top with the layer of mint and then the layer of chocolate.

Put the slice in the freezer for 15 minutes and then remove and cut into bite-sized pieces. Return to the freezer to further solidify.

Thaw slightly before eating.

This will keep in the freezer in an airtight container for up to 2 weeks.

SPINACH ICE CREAM

●WF ●DF ●GF ●VEG ●VG   SERVES 2–3

You may think that spinach and ice cream are the pair of ingredients most likely to end up on the cutting-room floor but, believe me, they make a lovely refreshing partnership. I've used bananas as the key ingredient in this creamy concoction. If you have overripe bananas, peel them and store them in the freezer so you can create ice cream whenever the mood strikes you. Please note that you do not need an ice-cream maker for this recipe.

2 peeled and frozen bananas

3 drops additive- and alcohol-free
    peppermint extract

1/2 cup frozen spinach

60 ml (2 fl oz/1/4 cup) additive-free
    coconut milk

6 drops stevia liquid, or sweetener of your
    choice (optional)

Place all the ingredients in a food processor and blend until smooth. Pour into a freezer-proof tray and freeze for 1 hour or until set.

For a creamier ice cream, increase the quantity of coconut milk.

Health Benefits

Bananas are a wonderfully rich source of potassium; a necessary electrolyte that encourages your body to burn carbohydrates as fuel and to maintain your acid base balance. With sodium being potassium's natural partner in crime, it pays to add potassium-rich foods to your diet. The Supercharged diet encourages the liberal use of Celtic sea salt to balance your sodium with your potassium. This is another way you can ensure your body is continually restoring and nourishing itself.

CARROT CAKE WITH COCONUT ICING

♠ WF ♥ GF ♣ SF ♦ VEG   MAKES 1 CAKE

This is a respectable carrot cake that embodies everything that a carrot cake should be. It is virtuous with lip-licking creamy frosting, filled with wholesome chunks of walnuts and a delicious mix of subtle sweetness and notes of spice.

To veganise: Substitute the eggs with 2 tablespoons ground or whole chia or flaxseeds soaked in 120 ml (3¾ fl oz) of water for 15 minutes.

150 g (5½ oz/1½ cups) almond meal, or gluten-free flour of your choice

60 g (2¼ oz/½ cup) raw chopped walnuts

½ teaspoon gluten-free baking powder

1 teaspoon bicarbonate of soda (baking soda)

¼ teaspoon Celtic sea salt

1 teaspoon ground cinnamon

½ teaspoon grated nutmeg

¾ teaspoon stevia powder

2 organic eggs, beaten

3 tablespoons organic butter, coconut oil or light olive oil

80 ml (2½ fl oz/⅓ cup) additive-free coconut milk

235 g (8½ oz/1½ cups) grated carrot

walnuts, to decorate (optional)

COCONUT ICING

120 g (4¼ oz/¾ cup) raw, unsalted cashews

300 ml (10½ fl oz) tinned coconut cream

finely grated zest and juice of ½ lemon

5 or 6 drops stevia, or sweetener of your choice

To make the coconut icing, place the cashews in a bowl, cover with filtered water and soak for 2 hours. Drain.

Place the cashews, half the coconut cream and the lemon zest and juice in a food processor and blitz for a few minutes. Slowly add more coconut cream until the consistency resembles crème fraîche – smooth, not runny, but not so thick as thickened cream. Once the desired consistency is reached, add the stevia liquid, drop by drop, until it reaches the desired sweetness.

Transfer to a bowl and add to the coldest section of your fridge for 30 minutes. Alternatively, put it in the freezer for 5–10 minutes to thicken.

Preheat the oven to 170°C (325°F/Gas 3) and grease an 18 cm (7 inch) round cake tin.

Put the almond meal, walnuts, baking powder, bicarbonate of soda, salt, cinnamon, nutmeg and stevia powder in a large bowl and stir to combine.

In a separate bowl, place the eggs, butter, coconut oil or light olive oil and coconut milk and whisk to combine.

Add the dry ingredients to the wet ingredients and fold through with a wooden spoon. Squeeze the excess water out of the carrots (using your hands is best) then add them to the bowl. Fold in lightly. Spoon the mixture into the prepared tin and bake for 45 minutes, or until the cake springs back when pressed in the centre.

Turn out onto a wire rack to cool. When the cake has cooled, spread the icing over the top using a knife or the back of a spoon and top with the walnuts.

This will keep, stored in an airtight container in the fridge, for up to 5 days.

SIDES, DIPS, SNACKS AND NIBBLES

Nip unhealthy snacking in the bud. Go beyond potato chips, peanuts and crudités, and indulge in speedy recipes that bring snacks back into foodies' good graces. From bite-sized pick-up-ables and nourishing sides, to dip-able veg and crunchable crackers, these portable feasts and customisable treats will have your entertaining and nibbling needs sorted.

CELERIAC FRIES

WF DF GF SF VEG VG   SERVES 2–3

While celeriac isn't the prettiest of veggies, its performance makes up in taste what it lacks in beauty. Crispy on the outside and soft on the inside, these fries make a delicious snack.

3 large celeriac, peeled and cut into 4 cm (1¹/2 inch) fries (see note)

1 tablespoon cold-pressed extra virgin olive oil

Celtic sea salt

freshly ground black pepper

Preheat the oven to 200°C (400°F/Gas 6).

Toss the celeriac fries in the olive oil and add a pinch of salt and pepper.

Place in a baking dish and roast for 30–35 minutes, turning them once or twice, until they are crispy.

NOTE: The thinner the fries, the crispier they will be.

BAKED ZUCCHINI FRIES

WF DF GF SF VEG   SERVES 2

These flavourful fries make the perfect snack and pair well with homemade mayo and a sprinkling of apple cider vinegar. For a cheesy version, add a tablespoon of nutritional yeast flakes.
To veganise: Use brown rice flour or almond meal in place of breadcrumbs.

cold-pressed extra virgin olive oil, for greasing

30 g (1 oz/¹/4 cup) superfine besan (chickpea flour)

¹/2 teaspoon paprika

pinch of Celtic sea salt

185 ml (6 fl oz/³/4 cup) almond milk

75 g (2¹/2 oz/1¹/4 cups) gluten-free breadcrumbs

2 zucchini (courgettes), cut into 4 cm (1¹/2 inch) chips

Preheat the oven to 220°C (425°F/Gas 7) and lightly grease a baking tray with olive oil.

Place the besan, paprika and salt in one bowl, the almond milk in another and the breadcrumbs in a third.

Dip the zucchini chips into the besan, then the milk, and lastly the breadcrumbs. Place in a single layer on the baking tray and bake for 30–35 minutes until golden, turning after 15 minutes.

⤜Supercharged Tip⤝

You could also use oregano, garam masala or turmeric for an anti-inflammatory boost.

FLAX CRACKERS

WF GF SF VEG   MAKES 12–14

Omega-rich flaxseeds and parmesan have teamed up to create the perfect party dipper.
To veganise: Flick the flax and flip over to page 125 and make the Nachos Chips.

cold-pressed extra virgin olive oil,
  for greasing

100 g (3¹/₂ oz/1 cup) flaxseed meal

50 g (1³/₄ oz/¹/₃ cup) grated
  parmesan cheese

¹/₂ teaspoon Celtic sea salt

125 ml (4 fl oz/¹/₂ cup) filtered water

Preheat the oven to 200°C (400°F/Gas 6) and grease
a baking tray with olive oil.

Combine all the remaining ingredients in a bowl and mix
well. Spoon the mixture onto the baking tray, pressing it
down firmly so the mixture is about 3 mm (¹/₈ inch) thick.

Cook in the oven for 15 minutes, then transfer the tray to
a wire rack to cool down and crisp up. Once crispy, use a
spatula to carefully lift the biscuit away from the tray and
break into bite-sized pieces.

These will keep in a sealed container for 2–3 weeks.

CHEESY STAR CRACKERS

WF DF GF SF VEG   MAKES 22 CRACKERS

To veganise: Substitute the egg with 1 tablespoon of ground flaxseed (or flaxseed meal) mixed
with 60 ml (2 fl oz/¹/₄ cup) of filtered water.

cold-pressed extra virgin olive oil,
  for greasing

200 g (7 oz/2 cups) almond meal

1 organic egg

2 tablespoons nutritional yeast flakes

1 tablespoon additive-free coconut milk

¹/₂ teaspoon Celtic sea salt, plus extra,
  for sprinkling

Preheat the oven to 170°C (325°F/Gas 3) and grease
a baking tray with olive oil.

Place all the remaining ingredients in a food processor
and blend until a smooth dough forms.

Place the dough on a sheet of baking paper and use a
rolling pin to roll out into a 30 x 20 cm (12 x 8 inch)
rectangle, about 3 mm (¹/₈ inch) thick. Using a dough
cutter, cut the dough into stars and transfer them to the
baking tray.

Sprinkle with a little salt and bake for 12–15 minutes,
or until crisp, turning after 6 minutes. Transfer the tray
to a wire rack for the crackers to cool down and crisp up.

The crackers will keep in an airtight container for up to
1 week, or longer if you keep them in the fridge.

SEA-SALTED FENNEL CHIPS

WF DF GF SF VEG VG   SERVES 2

These have a lovely caramelised flavour, and the aniseed from the fennel with the salt are a match made in heaven. You can also use parsnip if fennel is not in season — cut them into long, thin strips and bake the same way.

2 fennel bulbs

1 tablespoon cold-pressed extra virgin olive oil

pinch of Celtic sea salt

Preheat the oven to 180°C (350°F/Gas 4).

Trim the stalks and the base off the fennel. Cut the bulb in half, peeling the layers of leaves apart.

Place the leaves on a baking tray, drizzle with the olive oil and sprinkle lightly with salt.

Bake in the oven for 25 minutes, turning a few times and removing any smaller leaves that cook quickly. Cool for 15 minutes before serving.

HAPPY KALE CHIPS

WF DF GF SF VEG VG   SERVES 2

Kale is the word on the lips of every health-conscious foodie, and for good reason. Incredibly dense in nutrients and boasting anti-cancer and anti-inflammatory properties, this wonder-veg can also be made into just about anything, from chips to dips.

1 bunch of curly kale, stems removed, leaves torn into bite-sized pieces

1 tablespoon cold-pressed extra virgin olive oil

2 tablespoons nutritional yeast flakes

Preheat the oven to 200°C (400°F/Gas 6).

Combine the kale and oil in a large bowl and massage the oil into the kale.

Transfer to a baking tray, sprinkle with the nutritional yeast flakes and bake for 12 minutes.

These are best eaten straight out of the oven.

RED ONION BHAJIS WITH MINTED RAITA

●WF ♥GF ●SF ●VEG   MAKES 10–12

Bring a little bit of Bollywood into your kitchen with these exotic vegetarian morsels. Bhajis are the Indian version
of vegetable fritters, and are perfect as a colourful entrée or canapé at your next backyard soiree.

To veganise: Replace the yoghurt with the Cashew Nut Yoghurt on page 219.

120 g (4¼ oz/1 cup) superfine besan
  (chickpea flour)

¹/₂ teaspoon gluten-free baking powder

1 teaspoon chilli flakes

2 teaspoons curry powder

1 teaspoon ground coriander

1 teaspoon cumin

1 teaspoon turmeric

2 garlic cloves, crushed

2 cm (³/₄ inch) piece of ginger,
  finely chopped

Celtic sea salt and freshly ground
  black pepper

1 red onion, finely chopped

4 tablespoons extra virgin coconut oil
  or ghee, for frying

MINTED RAITA

130 g (4¹/₂ oz/¹/₂ cup) full-fat
  Greek yoghurt

2 tablespoons chopped mint

1 small garlic clove, crushed

To make the raita, mix all the ingredients together and place in a serving bowl.

To make the bhajis, sift the besan and baking powder into a large bowl. Add the spices, garlic and ginger and season with salt and pepper. Add 150 ml (5 fl oz) of cold water to make a thick batter, then add the onion and stir until it is well coated.

Heat the coconut oil in a heavy-based frying pan over medium heat. Add a tiny bit of mixture to test the oil temperature – if it bubbles, the oil is hot enough. Cooking several bhajis at a time, add a heaped tablespoon of mixture and shallow-fry until golden brown on each side; I like to form a tablespoon of the mixture into a patty before frying to help keep the shape.

Transfer to a paper towel to soak up the excess oil and cook the remaining batter.

Serve with the minted raita.

RED CAPSICUM AND HAZELNUT PESTO

●WF ●DF ●GF ●SF ●VEG ●VG   MAKES 2 CUPS

Homemade pesto is so easy to whip up yourself, that you'll soon be waving goodbye to the citric acid, preservatives, additives and the high-sodium hit that can accompany a large proportion of supermarket varieties.

1¹/2 **red capsicums (peppers), seeds and membrane removed, chopped**

3 garlic cloves, peeled and minced

2/3 **cup basil leaves**

1 tablespoon freshly grated ginger

2 tablespoons wheat-free tamari

1 tablespoon nutritional yeast flakes

juice and zest of 1 lemon

1 tablespoon apple cider vinegar

135 g (4³/4 oz/1 cup) lightly toasted hazelnuts

2 tablespoons cold-pressed extra virgin olive oil

pinch of Celtic sea salt and freshly ground pepper

Place all the ingredients in a food processor and whizz until it reaches the desired consistency.

This pesto will keep in a sealed jar in the fridge for up to 4 days.

⤷Supercharged Tip⤶

For a delicious variation, try substituting the hazelnuts with blanched almonds, or sunflower seeds and pepitas (pumpkin seeds).

BASIL PESTO

●WF ●DF ●GF ●SF ●VEG ●VG   MAKES 1 CUP

My man loves this recipe — he calls it pesto with a twist. Basil is packed with iron and magnesium, which improves circulation, and the essential oil eugenol provides anti-inflammatory effects similar to that of aspirin, making it as good for you as it is delicious.

160 g (5³/4 oz/1 cup) blanched almonds

2 garlic cloves, peeled

2 large handfuls of basil leaves

80 ml (2¹/2 fl oz/¹/3 cup) cold-pressed extra virgin olive oil

1 tablespoon freshly squeezed lemon juice

2 tablespoons nutritional yeast flakes

small pinch of Celtic sea salt

Place the almonds in a food processor and whizz until fine. Add the garlic and pulse, then add the basil and whizz again. With the motor running, slowly drizzle in the olive oil until you have the desired consistency, then add the lemon juice, yeast flakes and salt.

This pesto will keep in a sealed container in the fridge for up to 1 week and can be refreshed with an extra splash of extra virgin olive oil.

PASS THE BABA GHANOUSH

●WF ●DF ●GF ●SF ●VEG ●VG MAKES 1 CUP

Baba ghanoush makes a wonderful topping or dressing for salads, or a dip for crunchy veggies. You can also team it with quinoa, using it as a chunky sauce to add flavour.

1 large eggplant (aubergine)

65 g (2¼ oz/¼ cup) tahini

4 garlic cloves, finely chopped

Celtic sea salt, to taste

½ teaspoon ground cumin

125 ml (4 fl oz/½ cup) freshly squeezed lemon juice

chopped parsley, to garnish

Happy Kale Chips (see page 190) or gluten-free crackers, to serve

Preheat the oven grill (broiler) to medium.

Prick the eggplant with a fork and grill the eggplant for 30 minutes, turning frequently, until the skin is charred. Remove from the grill and set aside to cool.

Split the eggplant in half lengthways and scoop the pulp into a large bowl. Discard the skin.

Squeeze out the excess moisture from the eggplant pulp and then mix with the tahini, garlic, salt, cumin and lemon juice. Adjust the seasoning as necessary and scatter over the parsley leaves.

SPICED CARROT DIP

●WF ●DF ●GF ●SF ●VEG ●VG SERVES 2

Create a memorable mezze platter with this delicious and textural Middle Eastern–inspired dip bursting with zippy flavours.

2 teaspoons ground cumin

1 garlic clove, chopped

1 teaspoon grated ginger

Celtic sea salt and freshly ground black pepper

60 ml (2 fl oz/¼ cup) cold-pressed extra virgin olive oil

4 large carrots, coarsely chopped

vegetable crudités, Happy Kale Chips (see page 190) or gluten-free crackers, to serve

Preheat the oven to 180°C (350°F/Gas 4).

Mix the cumin, garlic, ginger, salt, pepper and half the olive oil together in a small bowl.

Place the carrot in a saucepan, cover with boiling water, and boil over high heat for 5 minutes.

Transfer the carrots to a baking tray and coat with the olive oil and spice mixture. Bake for 30–40 minutes or until lightly golden and tender.

Remove from the oven and set aside to cool.

Transfer to a food processor, add the remaining olive oil and blend until smooth.

Serve with vegetable crudités or gluten-free crackers.

TOASTED BROCCOLI AND HAZELNUT DIP

WF DF GF SF VEG VG   MAKES 2 CUPS

This delicious dip combines broccoli with aromatic hazelnuts, zingy lemon and herby basil. Your guests will be left in awe and begging for more.

125 ml (4 fl oz/1/2 cup) cold-pressed extra virgin olive oil, plus 1 tablespoon extra

1 large broccoli head, chopped into florets

1/4 cup basil leaves

pinch of chilli flakes

juice and zest of 1/2 lemon

75 g (21/2 oz/1/2 cup) hazelnuts

2 garlic cloves

1 tablespoon nutritional yeast flakes

Celtic sea salt

freshly ground black pepper

Add the 1 tablespoon of olive oil to a heavy-based frying pan over medium heat and stir-fry the broccoli for a few minutes, until browned.

Remove from the pan and let it cool slightly.

Combine all the ingredients in a blender or food processor with 2 tablespoons of filtered water. Pulse until well combined – if it feels too dry add one more teaspoon of olive oil.

LIVELY MINTED PEA DIP

WF DF GF SF VEG VG   MAKES 3 CUPS

420 g (143/4 oz/3 cups) fresh or frozen cooked green peas

juice of 1 small lemon

zest of 1 lemon

2 garlic cloves

1/4 cup packed mint leaves

2 tablespoons cold-pressed extra virgin olive oil

2 tablespoons tahini

1/4 teaspoon Celtic sea salt

freshly ground black pepper

Place all the ingredients in a food processor and blend on high.

Transfer to a bowl and serve garnished with a mint leaf.

⌇Supercharged Tip⌇

Store in an airtight container in the fridge for up to 3-4 days.

FUDGY BLACK BEAN BISCUITS

WF DF GF VEG VG   MAKES 10 LARGE BISCUITS

Beans absorb sweet flavours beautifully, and when blended, their smooth texture makes an ideal base for baked goods. Black beans in particular are loaded with protein and fibre, offering excellent health benefits to a normally nutritionless sweet treat. These fudgy biscuits will melt in your mouth with their gooey centres.

400 g (14 oz) tin black beans, rinsed and drained

2 tablespoons cold-pressed extra virgin olive oil

60 ml (2 fl oz/1/4 cup) rice malt syrup

2 tablespoons organic nut butter

2 tablespoons almond milk

4–5 tablespoons raw cacao powder

2 tablespoons almond meal

1/2 teaspoon ground cinnamon

1 teaspoon gluten-free baking powder

1/2 teaspoon Celtic sea salt

Preheat the oven to 180°C (350°F/Gas 4) and line a baking tray with baking paper.

Place the beans, olive oil, rice malt syrup, nut butter and almond milk in a food processor and blend until smooth. Add the remaining ingredients and whizz until it is smooth and thick.

Scoop 1 tablespoon at a time onto the baking tray and flatten a little. Bake for 20 minutes then transfer to a wire rack to cool.

These biscuits will keep for up to 4 days in an airtight container in the fridge.

ZUCCHINI ROLL UPS

WF   DF   GF   SF   VEG   VG   MAKES 15

There is nothing worse than being invited to a cocktail party, only to be presented with a choice of greasy, fried and tacky finger foods that make your insides feel terrible. Surprise your friends with these impressive spirals of zucchini filled with delicious vegan-friendly fillings.

2 zucchini (courgettes)

1/2 cup Sunflower Seed Cheese, see page 123

1/2 cup Basil Pesto, see page 194

1/2 cup Taco Filling, see page 123

Top and tail the zucchini and use a mandolin or vegetable peeler to peel long strips lengthways.

Place the zucchini strips on a chopping board or flat surface and add a teaspoon of the sunflower seed cheese, followed by the pesto and lastly the taco filling on the first 2 cm (3/4 inch). Roll up and secure with a toothpick.

Repeat until you have filled all your zucchini strips.

SWEET SPICED NUTS

WF   DF   GF   VEG   MAKES 4 CUPS

Move over chestnuts roasting on an open fire! Hot and spicy, with a hint of sweetness, you'll love these Christmassy-tasting nuts. Keep a stash on hand, pack them into bags and give them to your friends as homemade gifts. Store in jam jars and scatter on salads or cereals, too.

To veganise: Replace the coconut sugar and egg white with 80 ml (2½ fl oz/⅓ cup) of rice malt syrup.

100 g (3½ oz/⅔ cup) coconut sugar

2 teaspoons Celtic sea salt

2 teaspoons ground cinnamon

1½ teaspoons chilli powder

½ teaspoon ground allspice

½ teaspoon cayenne pepper

1 organic egg white, whisked until frothy

4 cups mixed nuts (see note)

Preheat the oven to 150°C (300°F/Gas 2) and line a baking tray with baking paper.

Whisk the coconut sugar, salt, spices and egg white together in a small bowl. Add the nuts and stir until they are coated in the egg mixture.

Transfer the nuts to the baking tray and bake for 40 minutes, turning after 20 minutes. Turn off the oven and let the nuts cool in the oven for another 20 minutes.

These will keep for 4 weeks in an airtight container.

NOTE: A good combination is almonds, walnuts, Brazil, hazelnuts, cashews and pistachios.

CINNAMON ROASTED CARROTS

WF   DF   GF   SF   VEG   VG   SERVES 2

Not only are carrots full of vitamin A, which is required for normal skin cell growth and development, they also have wonderful anti-inflammatory effects on ulcerous and inflamed tummies. You can rest assured that with every spoonful of these healing vegetables, you are bringing an abundance of health and vitality to your body.

2 carrots, thinly sliced

2 teaspoons extra virgin coconut oil

1/2 teaspoon ground cinnamon

pinch of Celtic sea salt

Preheat the oven to 220°C (425°F/Gas 7).

Place the carrot in a bowl and toss with the coconut oil and cinnamon.

Transfer to a baking tray in a single layer, season with salt and bake for 10–12 minutes.

Remove and enjoy their sweet flavour immediately.

SLOW-COOKED GREEN BEANS

WF DF GF SF VEG VG   SERVES 2

Vegetables don't need lengthy lists of exotic ingredients to make them a worthy component of a scrumptious feast. As in so many cases, this dish shows that less is more when showcasing superfood ingredients. These slow-cooked green beans are the perfect accompaniment to your lunch or dinner, and have a spectacular combination of nutrient-rich ingredients that'll really switch on your healing systems.

60 ml (2 fl oz/¼ cup) cold-pressed extra virgin olive oil

1 red onion, chopped

2 garlic cloves, sliced

150 g (5½ oz/2 cups) green beans, trimmed

12 tomatoes, chopped, or 800 g (1 lb 12 oz) tin additive-free tomatoes

2 tablespoons fresh or dried rosemary

400 ml (14 fl oz) vegetable stock

65 g (2¼ oz/½ cup) slivered almonds

Celtic sea salt

freshly ground black pepper

Heat the oil in a heavy-based saucepan over medium heat, then add the onion and garlic and sauté for 5 minutes. Add the beans, tomatoes, rosemary and stock, bring to the boil then reduce the heat to low and cook, covered, for 2 hours.

To serve, top with the almonds and season with salt and pepper.

COOCHY COODLES (CUCUMBER NOODLES) WITH CREAMY AVOCADO DRESSING

WF DF GF SF VEG VG   SERVES 2

Who needs refined, boiled-to-death noodles? With the right peeler, you can make your own raw noodles from a range of vegetables that are full of living nutrition. Cucumber noodles are refreshing and a great light lunch or side dish choice.

4 cucumbers

Creamy Avocado Dressing, see page 218

40 g (1¹/₂ oz/¹/₄ cup) pine nuts

Slice the cucumbers into noodles using a spiraliser or mandolin. Set aside in a colander for 20 minutes to remove any excess water.

Place the cucumber in a bowl and add the dressing. Put in the fridge to chill for 15 minutes.

Remove from the fridge and toss through the pine nuts for some added crunch.

SAGE MASHED CAULIFLOWER

⬤WF ⬤DF ⬤GF ⬤SF ⬤VEG ⬤VG   SERVES 4

My sage phase is currently in full swing and, due to its ivy-league nutritional profile, I like to swap out white potatoes for cauliflower when roasting or mashing. These fluffy and light veg are an ideal accompaniment to main meals, or a smashing and comforting meal in a bowl.

375 g (13 oz/3 cups) cauliflower florets

1 tablespoon sage leaves, roughly chopped

1 tablespoon organic almond butter

1 teaspoon Celtic sea salt

1/2 teaspoon freshly ground black pepper

pinch of nutmeg

Line a bamboo steamer with baking paper and steam the cauliflower over a saucepan of gently simmering water for 6–8 minutes, or until soft. Remove from the heat and combine all the ingredients in a food processor. Pulse until completely mashed but the consistency is not runny.

Transfer to a bowl and serve.

INDIAN WHOLE ROASTED CAULIFLOWER

⬤WF ⬤DF ⬤GF ⬤SF ⬤VEG ⬤VG   SERVES 2

This dish adorns the blank canvas of the whole cauliflower with a magnificent mix of colourful, aromatic and anti-inflammatory ingredients.

1 large cauliflower, washed

1/4 cup coriander (cilantro) leaves, for garnish

MARINADE

4 garlic cloves, crushed

1 tablespoon turmeric

80 ml (2 1/2 fl oz/1/3 cup) freshly squeezed lemon juice

80 ml (2 1/2 fl oz/1/3 cup) cold-pressed extra virgin olive oil

1 teaspoon Celtic sea salt

2 tablespoons nutritional yeast flakes

125 ml (4 fl oz/1/2 cup) coconut cream

Preheat the oven to 180°C (350°F/Gas 4).

Place all the marinade ingredients in a jug and stir to combine.

Place the cauliflower in a large bowl and spoon over the marinade, ensuring the cauliflower is well coated.

Place the cauliflower on a baking tray and roast for 45–55 minutes, until tender and crispy.

Garnish with the coriander and serve.

SAVOURY SMASHED ROOT VEGETABLES

WF DF GF SF VEG VG   SERVES 4

Later 'taters. Mash isn't just all about spuds. Served either as a light meal on its own or as a side, this tri-coloured bowl of primitive, hulk-inspiring nourishment will have you at hello.

1 small turnip, peeled and cut into chunks

1 medium parsnip, peeled and cut into chunks

1 medium sweet potato, peeled and cut into chunks

1 large carrot, peeled and cut into chunks

2 tablespoons cold-pressed extra virgin olive oil

80 ml (2½ fl oz/⅓ cup) additive-free coconut milk

2 garlic cloves, sliced

2 tablespoons nutritional yeast flakes

pinch of Celtic sea salt

freshly ground black pepper

Place the turnip and parsnip in a large saucepan. Cover with water and bring to the boil over medium heat. Boil for 10 minutes, then add the remaining vegetables and boil for a further 20–30 minutes, or until the vegetables are soft.

In a separate, small saucepan, simmer the olive oil, coconut milk and garlic over low heat for 5 minutes.

Drain the vegetables and place in a food processor with the coconut milk mixture and nutritional yeast flakes and pulse briefly, so the vegetables are still chunky. Season to taste with salt and pepper.

A SIDE ORDER OF GREEN BEANS AND SPINACH

WF DF GF SF VEG VG   SERVES 4

Although we all realise the benefits of veggies in our diets, there is often a disconnect between what we know and what we actually do. This recipe pairs two high-powered green veg to culminate in a crunchy flavour-popping dish.

1 tablespoon cold-pressed extra virgin olive oil

1 onion, chopped

1 large garlic clove, crushed

150 g (5½ oz/1 cup) green beans, trimmed

2 bunches of English spinach leaves

1 tomato, chopped

1 teaspoon thyme leaves

1 teaspoon basil leaves

2 tablespoons apple cider vinegar

Celtic sea salt

freshly ground black pepper

Heat the olive oil in a large frying pan over medium heat. Add the onion and garlic and cook for 3–5 minutes, or until the onion softens and browns slightly. Add the beans and cook for 10 minutes, stirring frequently so it doesn't burn. Add the spinach and tomato and cook for a further 2–3 minutes. Lastly, add the herbs, 60 ml (2 fl oz/¼ cup) of filtered water and the apple cider vinegar.

To serve, season with salt and pepper.

ORIENTAL SPINACH

WF DF GF VEG VG   SERVES 2

Get acquainted with your inner herbivore with this dish that provides instant gratification. It's an easy and quick-to-make recipe, bursting with goodness and packed with zesty oriental flavours.

3 handfuls of baby spinach

MARINADE

1 tablespoon flaxseed oil

1 tablespoon apple cider vinegar

1 tablespoon wheat-free tamari

1 teaspoon rice malt syrup

1 teaspoon minced garlic

1 spring onion (scallion), thinly sliced

Combine the marinade ingredients in a small bowl and mix well.

Place the spinach leaves in a salad bowl, pour over the marinade and chill in the fridge for 15 minutes before serving.

DOLLOPS, DRESSINGS AND SAUCES

Turn up the sauciness and flavour of your dishes, and relish in plant-powered dollops to take a meal from drab to fab. Wave goodbye to vegan mayonnaise substitutes and enjoy Creamed Spinach Sauce, Mint Chutney and Lemon and Garlic Aïoli. Cultivate your veggies and bring them into the spotlight.

RANCH DRESSING

●WF ●DF ●GF ●VEG ●VG   MAKES 1¼ CUPS

50 g (1¾ oz/⅓ cup) raw, unsalted cashews

2 tablespoons freshly squeezed lemon juice

1 tablespoon apple cider vinegar

1 teaspoon rice malt syrup

125 ml (4 fl oz/½ cup) almond milk

1 tablespoon tahini

¼ cup parsley leaves

2 teaspoons chopped chives

1 garlic clove, crushed

¼ teaspoon sugar-free mustard

big pinch of Celtic sea salt

freshly ground black pepper, to taste

Soak the cashews for 2 hours in filtered water. Rinse, drain and pat dry.

Place all the ingredients in a food processor and blend to the desired consistency.

This dressing will keep in an airtight container in the fridge for up to 5 days.

MINT CHUTNEY

●WF ●DF ●GF ●VEG ●VG   MAKES 1 CUP

2 cups mint leaves

1 cup coriander (cilantro) leaves

1 shallot, minced

juice and zest of 1 lime

60 ml (2 fl oz/¼ cup) coconut cream

1 tablespoon cold-pressed extra virgin olive oil

pinch of Celtic sea salt

1 tablespoon rice malt syrup, or
   ¼ teaspoon stevia powder, or 6 drops
   stevia liquid

1 tablespoon apple cider vinegar

Place all the ingredients in a food processor and pulse until well combined.

⊱ Supercharged Tip ⊰

This can be used as a side dressing, but it's also delicious as a dip. It will keep for up to 5 days in the fridge.

CASHEW SOUR CREAM

WF DF GF SF VEG VG   MAKES 1 CUP

155 g (5$^{1}/_{2}$ oz/1 cup) raw, unsalted cashews

2 teaspoons apple cider vinegar

2 tablespoons freshly squeezed lemon juice, plus 1 teaspoon extra

1$^{1}/_{2}$ teaspoons nutritional yeast flakes

$^{1}/_{4}$ teaspoon Celtic sea salt

Soak the cashews for 2 hours in filtered water. Rinse and drain.

Place all the ingredients in a food processor with 125 ml (4 fl oz/$^{1}/_{2}$ cup) of filtered water and blend until smooth. You may need to add a little more filtered water to reach your desired consistency.

This will keep for 2–3 days in an airtight container in the fridge.

TAHINI AND TURMERIC DRESSING

WF DF GF SF VEG VG   MAKES 125 ML (4 FL OZ/$^{1}/_{2}$ CUP)

For a moreish flavour hit to spark up raw veggies, embrace this blissful dressing. Not only does it boast yummification super-powers, it's also packed with the anti-inflammatory, anti-cancer and antioxidant properties of turmeric.

65 g (2$^{1}/_{4}$ oz/$^{1}/_{4}$ cup) tahini

2 tablespoons wheat-free tamari

1 tablespoon turmeric

Place all the ingredients in a food processor with 60 ml (2 fl oz/$^{1}/_{4}$ cup) of filtered water and blend until smooth. Transfer to a glass jar and refrigerate for 30 minutes to let the flavours meld. This will keep for 4–5 days in an airtight container in the fridge.

LEMON AND GARLIC AÏOLI

WF DF GF SF VEG VG   MAKES $^{3}/_{4}$ CUP

80 g (2$^{3}/_{4}$ oz/$^{1}/_{2}$ cup) raw, unsalted cashews

2 garlic cloves

pinch of Celtic sea salt

juice of 1 lemon

1 tablespoon filtered water

Place the cashews in a bowl, cover with filtered water and soak for 2 hours. Drain.

Place all the ingredients in a food processor and blend until creamy.

This will keep for 4–5 days in an airtight container in the fridge.

CREAMY AVOCADO DRESSING

WF DF GF SF VEG VG   MAKES 125 ML (4 FL OZ/½ CUP)

Avocados are uniquely decadent dwellers in the plant world. Silky, buttery and smooth, they supply high fulfilment, even when eaten alone. Blended into a dressing, they offer your salad a gorgeous pop of yellowy green and a burst of good fats that will moisturise your body from the inside out.

1 avocado, peeled and stone removed

1 heaped teaspoon cumin powder

juice of 1 large lime

1 teaspoon lime zest

big pinch of Celtic sea salt

1 tablespoon cold-pressed extra virgin olive oil

Blend all the ingredients except the olive oil with 2 tablespoons of filtered water in a food processor until smooth. With the motor still running, add the olive oil very slowly in a thin stream until the desired creaminess is reached.

This will keep for 3–4 days in an airtight container in the fridge.

CREAMED SPINACH SAUCE

WF DF GF SF VEG VG   MAKES 250 ML (9 FL OZ/1 CUP)

With a little creativity, you can find innumerable ways to sneak more veggies into your diet. This scrumptiously wicked creamed spinach sauce will deliver maximum nutrition to a variety of meals without any telltale bitterness.

2 tablespoons extra virgin coconut oil

1 red onion, finely chopped

3 garlic cloves, crushed

1 red chilli, thinly sliced

3 bunches of English spinach leaves

Celtic sea salt

freshly ground black pepper, to taste

125 ml (4 fl oz/½ cup) additive-free coconut milk

Heat the coconut oil in a frying pan over medium heat and sauté the onion, garlic and chilli for 5 minutes, or until soft. Add the spinach and stir-fry until wilted. Season and add the coconut milk. Stir well to combine and simmer for 3–5 minutes to reduce the sauce before serving.

This will keep for 4–5 days in an airtight container in the fridge.

VINAIGRETTE

WF DF GF VEG VG   MAKES 205 ML (7¹/4 FL OZ)

125 ml (4 fl oz/¹/2 cup) apple cider vinegar

80 ml (2¹/2 fl oz/¹/3 cup) cold-pressed extra virgin olive oil

1 teaspoon wheat-free tamari

1 teaspoon rice malt syrup, or sweetener of your choice

Place all the ingredients in a jam jar and shake until well combined.

This will keep for 4–5 days in an airtight container in the fridge.

CASHEW DRESSING

WF DF GF SF VEG VG   MAKES 375 ML (13 FL OZ/1¹/2 CUPS)

310 g (11 oz/2 cups) raw, unsalted cashews

1 tablespoon freshly squeezed lemon juice

1 teaspoon Celtic sea salt

5 tablespoons nutritional yeast flakes

Soak the cashews for 2 hours in filtered water. Rinse, drain and pat dry.

Place all the ingredients in a food processor with 185 ml (6 fl oz/³/4 cup) of filtered water and whizz, scraping down the side as you go.

You may need to add a little more filtered water to reach the desired consistency.

This dressing will keep for up to 5 days in the fridge.

CASHEW NUT YOGHURT

WF DF GF VEG VG   MAKES 375 ML (13 FL OZ/1¹/2 CUPS)

155 g (5¹/2 oz/1 cup) raw, unsalted cashews

400 ml (14 fl oz) additive-free coconut milk, chilled

2 tablespoons white chia seeds

2 teaspoons alcohol-free vanilla extract

2 tablespoons freshly squeezed lemon juice

2 tablespoons rice malt syrup

Soak the cashews for 2 hours in filtered water. Rinse, drain and pat dry.

Place the cashews, coconut milk, chia and vanilla in a food processor and blend until smooth. Add the lemon juice and rice malt syrup and whizz again until smooth. Pour into a jar and refrigerate overnight to thicken.

This will keep for up to 5 days in an airtight container in the fridge.

INDEX

ACKNOWLEDGMENTS

There are so many people I would like to thank for bringing this book into your hands. A book is seldom the effort of one author and this book has been brought to you by a large team of hardworking and dedicated people.

Firstly I would like to thank the team at Murdoch Books, and in particular my publisher, the beautiful and inspiring Diana Hill. Diana has always believed in my potential and vision for Supercharged Food. I'd also like to thank the wonderful Christine Farmer for her invaluable insight and experience and for providing the platform for me to spread my message. Thanks to my super smart editors, Virginia Birch and Claire Grady, and to Alex Frampton for the stunning design. Thank you also to Robert Gorman, Sue Hines and Hugh Ford for all their support.

Thanks so much to the shoot team who really brought this book to life creatively: super chef Grace Campbell, talented photographers Steve Brown and Cath Muscat and gorgeous stylist Sarah O'Brien.

So many wonderful people have supported me whilst writing this book and have changed the trajectory of my life. Thank you to my friends and colleagues who have been so generous with their time and advice: Louise Cornege; Juliet Potter; Howard Porter; Georgie Bridge; Natalie Hostetler; Lise Hearns; Cindy Luken; Jessica Lowe; Pia Larsen; Marrianne Little; Meredith Gaston; Grahame Grassby; Mike Conway; Hayley Dutton; Kim Cotton; Sebastian Thaw; Erica Luiz; Monique Richards; Martin Chalk and Cindy Sciberras. Thanks to Alexx Stuart for her dessert recipes.

A very big thank you to my amazing family: Alex von Kotze; Roxy; Arizona; Carol; Lorraine; Clive; and Ben for their love and support. To my beautiful daughter, Tamsin, thank you for making me see life through fresh eyes and for never failing to give me not-so-gentle critiques on recipes. A big cuddle to my best friend Cashew for always being by my side. To my partner, Justin, thank you for your never-ending support and love and for always being in my corner.

For more delicious recipes, articles and information, please visit my website superchargedfood.com.

Socialise with me
share: superchargedfood.com
like: facebook.com/superchargedfood
follow: twitter.com/LeeSupercharged
blog: supercharged1.wordpress.com
insta: instagram.com/leesupercharged
link: linkedin.com/in/leesupercharged
watch: youtube.com/leeholmes67

Lee